BORN OF METAL

Rings of the Inconquo, Book 1

A.L. KNORR
A.D. SCHNEIDER

Edited by
GEORGIA CARTER MATHERS

Intellectually Promiscuous Press

This story is written in British English and edited using the Chicago Manual of Style.

Created with Vellum

Prologue

He didn't like the desert.

A true Brit, Professor James Lowe would take the murky English summer and foggy London night over the brain-cooking heat of the desert. In jolly ol' England, the sun was polite enough to step behind a curtain of clouds now and then, even in the humid summer, but not here. Here the sun was utterly merciless and uncomfortably close. Hot, yet dry. It was odd, the sensation of being slowly mummified alive. He wondered if his body had forgotten how to sweat.

He passed under the shadow of an immense sandstone idol, cleaning his spectacles for the hundredth time. The sun stabbed down through a wide fissure in the chamber ceiling, casting the stonework in sharp relief.

"Perhaps the sun wasn't so abominable when people were still offering sacrifices to it." He squinted up at the stone figure staring blankly down with an ibis's sad eyes. The grunts and thuds of the excavation team echoed from the shrine.

"That fellow is Thoth, not Horus or Ra." Lowe's

colleague, Prof Harold Weston, was perpetually cheery in spite of the torturous desert conditions. "He was not a sky or sun god, but a god of knowledge and craftsmanship."

Lowe stifled an irritated retort.

"Naturally." Lowe was thankful his sunburn hid the blush rising in his cheeks. He wasn't embarrassed by his seeming ignorance, or at least not much. Keeping up the façade was necessary to allay suspicion. Lowe was not an Egyptologist like Weston, but knew full well who the idol depicted, because he'd been secretly searching for the Sons of the Bronze Scroll for many years. It wouldn't do for Weston to know his little secret, though it would have been delightful to knock the grotesquely optimistic grin off the man's broad, tanned face.

"It appears your team found this after the soldiers." Lowe dragged his gaze over the spent rifle casings and cigarette stubs littering the floor.

"Yes, quite," the archaeologist chuckled as he continued down the hallway, scattering a few brass shells into the dark recesses beyond the sun's light. "Seems the lads cracked the whole thing like an egg with a mortar blast and used it as a redoubt when the enemy counterattacked. Bloody awful show by the sound of it, but when the smoke cleared, they were quick enough to let us in."

Lowe had wondered at the dark stains he'd spied here and there, but hadn't asked. Turned out he was right.

They were near the rear of the chamber, and the split in the roof had narrowed to a final spike of sunlight. Weston and Lowe produced torches, and with a pair of dull clicks, the back of the space was bathed in orange light. Two large blocks of basalt jutted forwards from the back wall, a narrow space left between them. In that gap, something glittered, and Lowe forgot about the sun, the sand and even Weston's annoying good humour.

The two men shared a silent moment of mutual thrill, and then — like two schoolboys — nearly raced to the gap. The light of their torches made glimmering shapes dance and twinkle. The gap was just large enough for a man to slide through sideways to reach the small chamber beyond.

Lowe began to squeeze through then checked himself, looking back at Weston and hanging halfway out the rocky crevice. "I expect you've already been through?"

The archaeologist shook his head. "Afraid not, ol' boy." Weston smiled sheepishly and patted his considerable belly. "I was afraid of damaging the site. I studied what I could from here."

"And?" Lowe grunted as he wriggled deeper.

"It's not ancient Egyptian or anything of that sort, and that places it firmly outside of my realm of expertise." Weston shrugged. "I contacted some mutual friends, and learning you were in Alexandria, I thought what a capital opportunity. A scholar of multiple Near Eastern peoples and artefacts."

Lowe felt guilty then for what little value he'd placed on Weston. At the very least, the man was humble enough to know when to get help, and that was more than most learned men could manage.

"I can't thank you enough," Lowe muttered abashedly, "but you should be the first …"

Lowe's voice tapered off as Weston's head wagged good naturedly. "Not at all." He waved his free hand before patting his round stomach with another chuckle. "Go on ahead. I'm confident I'll not fit, and my reputation would be in tatters if I got stuck."

Lowe didn't need further prompting.

It *was* an awfully tight fit, as it turned out. More than once he felt a flutter of near panic as he inched along. He was far thinner than Weston but still lost more than one button in the journey. With a final gasp, he was through.

The room was pitch black except where the light of the torch fell, and for a long moment, he stood with that light pooling around his feet.

"Steady," Lowe muttered quietly, bracing himself for what might come next.

Years of searching hung on this moment.

Weston's voice drifted in from the outer chamber as a hoarse whisper. The flash of his torch wove in and out of view.

"Are you through?"

Lowe let out a low breath before calling over his shoulder. "I'm through, and no worse for wear."

"What do you see?"

The weight of the question settled on him like a lead blanket as he raised the beam of his torch. Inch by inch, the light revealed an immense bas-relief worked in bronze, silver and gold. Part diorama, part historical record, its lines and symmetries were distinctly Sumerian. The entire relief was framed in an amalgam of cuneiform and hieroglyph he'd never seen before.

Centring the entire edifice was a simple abstract recreation of an engraved scroll. Lowe's fingers ran across the smooth contours of the raised lines, depressing a section here and there. There was a deep thump and a soft rumbling sound.

"Lowe!" Weston's voice was shrill. "What do you see?"

The bas-relief began to shift and rearrange. A smile spread across his face.

"The answer," he whispered to himself. "The answer to all the riddles." He picked up the welded gauntlet of four rings and stuffed them into his pocket.

Chapter One

I checked the status icon next to Uncle Irshad's smiling face.

Grey: inactive.

I gave a long, sputtering sigh and sank back into what passed for my love seat, fingers tightening around a cup of cooling tea.

"No news is good news," I told myself, but I hated the patronising words as soon as I said them.

For Uncle Irshad Bashir — like so many others in Sudan — no news could just as easily mean something truly terrible. Militias, famine and plague had taken more than one could imagine from so many people in the homeland of my parents. Though Uncle Iry was always smiling during our chats, even he couldn't pretend that things weren't bad. After all, it was why my parents left.

The older I grew, the more I marvelled at my parents' bravery. Leaving Sudan and everything they knew in the hope of a better life for themselves and their unborn child (that'd be yours truly) took a megaton of faith and guts.

Glaring at the icon, I narrowed my eyes and loosed a

telepathic request that he come on-line. The grey disc sat there in mute rebellion. I gave up in disgust. I checked the time — 1:20am — and groaned.

Tomorrow is going to be the utter pits.

I should've gone to bed hours ago, but I wouldn't sleep well unless I knew Uncle Iry was all right. I didn't dare hope he'd gotten hired, but maybe that was because I was trying not to think about work. My gaze wandered across my tiny flat to where my work jacket hung on a peg beside my bed. My smiling face grinned from the ID badge clipped to the lapel.

Bashir, Ibukun

Collections

British Museum

"A better life for you, Ibby," my mother had said one night. "A better life where you can grow up without fear of bad men with guns."

"You never met, Adrian Shelton, *'um*," I had muttered, using the Arabic for the word mum. "There are times I'd rather face bad men with guns."

My eyes roved past the grey icon before settling on the pinched window that revealed only the wall of the neighbouring building.

I wasn't serious, of course, but my supervisor was not to be trifled with. Adrian Shelton was a terribly demanding and critical man. He seemed to take particular satisfaction in scrutinising everything I did. I had little option except to adopt the old stiff upper lip. I didn't just need the pitiful pay packet, the internship was the best shot I had in getting a real job once I graduated university. My whole future hung on making Dr Shelton happy, and I wasn't convinced the man even knew *how* to be happy.

More important even than my future was my uncle's life, which depended on my success. Every day he stayed in

Sudan was another day his life was at risk. Putting an end to that risk meant money. Money I could earn if I finally got a good paying job, ideally (if I could dare to dream) with the Museum of Natural History.

I swallowed another sad sigh and got up with my now cold cup of tea. Hopping over a pile of folded laundry on my way to the countertop, which made the whole of my kitchenette, I turned the electric kettle on and stared at the blue light as the contraption began to rumble and hiss.

Like tyres on wet streets. Like that night.

My arms wrapped around my chest reflexively as the thought rocked me. It was nearly nine months since a lorry took a wet street corner too fast, sending both my parents to an early grave. They'd gone out to celebrate my mother getting a job as a nurse, the very occupation she'd had for years in Sudan before coming to London. It had taken her nearly two decades, but she was finally going to do the job she was born for.

My father had known my mother wanted to tell me the news herself, but when I'd called that night, he couldn't help himself.

He'd blurted out, "She got it, Ibby! She got the job!" before I'd even said a word.

He'd apologised to my mother immediately afterwards and handed the phone to her, but she was too happy to let his outburst spoil things. My father was like my uncle, ready smiles and easy laughs, a man who wore his big heart on his sleeve. Mother was softer, quieter, yet somehow stronger for it. "Yes, Ibby," she had said in her low, smooth voice. "I'm a nurse again."

It was one of the last things my mother ever said to me. That and their plans to bring my Uncle Iry to the UK, with money from the new job.

Now I was Uncle Iry's best hope. His only hope.

Still hugging myself, I glanced at the laptop screen. My tired eyes skidded over the status icon but everything snapped into focus when it flashed.

Green: active.

My tea and the kettle forgotten, I vaulted over the laundry and dodged a cast-off pair of shoes as I lunged for the laptop. Jamming the headset into place with one hand, I frantically worked the mouse with the other. Uncle Iry had to pay for each minute he was on-line at a small internet café, so every second was precious.

The status bar showed a connection being made, and my feet did a little dance of joy.

A few seconds later a window popped up. A dark, bare scalp and forehead lurked beneath a view of the ceiling with peeling plaster and glaring fluorescent lights.

"Ibby? Are you there?" My uncle's deep voice came through the headset with only a little distortion crackling over his accented words.

"Try pointing the camera down, *a'am*," I suggested. My uncle had asked we always talk in English so he could practise, but I couldn't help slipping a little Arabic in here and there.

The view in the chat window shifted, pixelating, then resolved into Irshad's handsome face, complete with a well-kept beard and our family's bronze eyes. As the screen sharpened, he wore a frown of concentration. I couldn't help noticing how hollow his cheeks looked and the deepening lines around his mouth and eyes. These all vanished when he smiled that immense grin. My heart ached. He reminded me of my father so much.

Every day costs him a little more.

"What's a good girl like you doing up at a time like dis?" He sounded grave, but he didn't put his smile away.

"I couldn't sleep," I lied, trying not to rub at my

burning eyes. "I hoped you'd make an appearance. It's been almost a week, *a'am-mi.*"

My uncle's expression became contrite, and he nodded. "I'm sorry, Ibby, I should have got in touch earlier. Things have been … difficult."

I clenched my fist and ground my knuckles into my thigh in shame for guilting him. Uncle Iry, along with living in one of the most unsettled regions in Sudan, had to walk many miles for internet. He only had time in the late evenings because he was either looking for or doing what work he could find. Though he didn't say it, I knew he was exhausted.

"No, I'm sorry, it's just …" I bit my lip, fighting to find words and trying to keep the tears at bay. The last thing my uncle needed was to spend his precious few minutes watching me weep. He'd endured enough of that when my parents first passed.

"But, I have good news, Ibby! Very good news!"

Uncle Iry coming to the rescue even from thousands of miles away.

I forced my voice to steady. "Really? Don't keep me in suspense. Don't you know it's late?"

He chuckled, his smile returning in force.

"A company is expanding and needs construction workers. Their foreman was looking for men with welding experience, so I have work for the next few months. Possibly longer!"

This wasn't good news; it was great news. Once upon a time, my uncle and father had worked as automotive mechanics in a garage in Nyala. When my father expressed a hope to take his newly pregnant bride to the UK, my uncle had used what little savings he'd had to make it happen. Shortly thereafter, the violence and the swelling tide of displaced peoples had driven him from Nyala back to their home village in the scrublands. It took years for the brothers to reconnect after the chaos, and both of them had hardly been able to scrape together enough to live. For years now, Uncle Iry has squeaked by, taking whatever work he could. A job like this, skilled and with potential for extended work, was very rare.

But something caught my attention, and I felt a tremor of suspicion twist in my belly.

"A'am, you said company. But what company? What are you building?"

Uncle Iry's smile weakened a little, and he wagged a finger across the screen. "Now, Ibby, remember, English only."

He was stalling. The twist in my stomach tightened into a knot. "Uncle … "

The smile shifted into an embarrassed grin that might have won me over if I hadn't known what was coming next.

"Greater Nile Petrol. We are expanding some of the oil rigs."

The knot became a weight that took out the bottom of my stomach. "Greater Nile! Oh, Iry, no." I sank into the love seat.

"Ibby, this is still good news. It will be safe, I promise."

Iry has always been an honest man, but in this moment, he was lying. Not only was the GNP notorious for their callous working conditions, but they were a favourite target for whatever band of armed thugs was roaming the area. He couldn't promise me he'd be safe because oil rigs throughout Sudan were one of the most dangerous places he could be.

There was no stopping the tears welling in my eyes this time.

"I know it is scary, Ibby, but if I'm kept on, I'm that much closer to rejoining my family."

He meant me. The brutality of life in Sudan had taken everything from us.

I tried to shove away the thoughts, the guilt, the wishes, but they came in like a flood. It was beyond unfair. It was utterly cruel, and I was powerless. Nothing I could say, nothing I could do was going to keep him from those oil rigs, because nothing mattered as much to either of us as being together.

Crying wasn't going to help. Uncle Iry needed me to be strong, no matter what. I brushed away my tears and smoothed out my voice. "And you'll be that much closer to a complimentary tour of the Museum of Natural History given by your niece, where she'll soon be working."

The last words caught in my throat, but I forced them out, a bright promise I'd do anything to keep.

Uncle Iry's brilliant smile was worth it. "I can't wait for that day, Ibby. Tell me, how is the internship going?"

Chapter Two

The alarm buzzed angrily near my ear. I swatted clumsily at my phone, knocking it onto the floor, where the buzz became a rattle.

Half-groaning, half-snarling I threw myself over the edge of my mattress to snag the nasty thing. Sleep-numbed fingers fumbled at the snooze button as one bleary eye glared at the screen. The alarm quit as the display kicked my sluggish brain into action.

7:30am

I was late. Very late.

I didn't notice what time I'd logged off after talking to Uncle Iry, but it had been much longer than usual. His new job with Greater Nile had made him confident enough to splurge, and how could I say no? When we finally logged off, I'd barely managed to remove the headset before collapsing onto my mattress.

I sat up, rubbing at my face and willing my sleep-deprived brain to work. Was there any way to get to work on time?

On a good day, I'd be out the door by 6:40am to reach

Mile End by 7am, where I could take the Central line to Tottenham Court Road. That put me inside the museum by 7:40am. Early enough even for a miserable busybody like Shelton.

On a desperate day, I'd scramble to Stepney Green, ride the Hammersmith & City line to Liverpool Street, take Central to Holborn and then run like mad. That would give me a chance of coming in the back doors, where Eddy, the porter, would let me in on the sly. I could swipe in and get down to Collections before Shelton came to berate me. When he'd stick his beaky nose into the sorting room, I'd greet him with a cheery "good morning!" and he'd slink away to criticise someone else.

I was well past that point.

My hands slid from my face to my temples where I squeezed an ache that ran from my scalp to somewhere behind my eyes.

I was going to be late. Shelton was going to tell me off, that glimmer of hideous joy in his eyes the whole time. There was no way around it.

With one more groan, I set to getting ready, thankful my hair was already up in braids from the night before. I set the kettle to boil and took a shower that was too fast to be either warm or relaxing, before setting my coffee to percolate. The good thing about working in Collections is that my wardrobe choices are simple. Dark slacks, an understated top and a drab uniform jacket with an ID badge hanging from the lapel.

I nabbed my bag and coffee in one fell swoop and didn't bother to check myself in the mirror. Shelton would have to have it out with me as I was.

Walking at a brisk stride to Mile End, I descended into the incessantly loud and busy world of the London Underground. The soundtrack of east London's poorer district was a mishmash of centuries-old cockney drawls among Hindi dialects and a host of other tongues. It was the background music of my entire life. My parents had never gotten used to it, but I was a born Londoner. The hum of the underground was like an old wool blanket. Scratchy in places, but oh so familiar.

I let myself fall into that blanket as I took a textbook out of my bag. Commuters around me texted, read, listened to music. London's underground even had wi-fi these days for those who bought service from the bigger telecom companies. I thumbed through my books while the Central line rolled on. I examined an explanation of how metal artefacts can tell an observant archaeologist not only 'when' something was made, but 'where,' right down to the hill or crag it was mined from. This in turn revealed much about the people who made it, their technology, their place in human history. A few trace elements here, a few surveys there and a single item could reshape what we understood about people alive hundreds or thousands of years ago.

It was like magic, and I loved it.

It was why I was interning at the museum but also why I was frustrated to be shunted into Collections instead of Cataloguing. I wanted to examine artefacts, assess their traits, check their provenance, even put something under an electron microscope. Rocks, metals, stones — they'd fascinated me since I was a child, and the older, the better. As I'd matured, my interests honed. Detective work, almost forensic intersection of archaeology and geology, had fascinated me since the beginning of grammar school.

In Collections, I organised boxes and punched numbers into a computer. Dry as dust. The museum's selection of antiquities was vast, and they constantly rotated exhibits from their archives to the floor and back again. It was the job of my department to handle the paperwork, ensuring nothing was misfiled or lost. It wasn't that the work didn't have significance. After all, misplacing a box full of ancient artefacts was tragic, but it was the sort of work a trained monkey could do. Check the number on your screen, check the number on the box, check the seal, stamp it. Repeat.

I was nearing a year of this drudgery without ever getting to actually handle the artefacts. If it weren't for some of my classes, I might not have experience with them at all.

I looked up from my book, pushing away gloomy thoughts, to see my stop was next. I checked my phone for the time.

8:22am

I packed up, squared my shoulders and hopped off at Tottenham Court Road. I was going to face Adrian Shelton with my head held high.

That attitude lasted until I reached the security desk at the front staff entrance. Tariq, one of the two porters stationed there, gave a pitying glance as I swiped in.

"Careful, Miss Ibby. Dr Shelton is on the prowl, and he is hungry."

My shoulders sagged. I didn't think of myself as a pushover. After all, I grew up in the East End, but exhaustion paired with latent anxiety over Uncle Iry was taking its toll. Shelton suddenly seemed like Goliath, and I was no David.

A rat of anxiety scampered through my mid-section as I glanced around the lobby and leaned towards Tariq. He caught my eye and rocked forwards to share in a brief conspiracy.

"Any chance you know where he's prowling right now?" I murmured.

Tariq looked sideways at his fellow porter, a man we knew only as McPhee, who shrugged and returned to staring at his monitor. Tariq inched a little closer.

I wondered randomly — *is my coffee breath as bad as the porter's?*

"He asked us to inform him the second you showed up, then he made for the administrative offices." His voice dropped to a whisper. "Probably sharpening his canines. You know how much he loves blood, fresh from the jugular."

I fought the urge to stare towards the left-hand corridor in dread anticipation. My voice went up an octave. "When was that?"

Tariq looked over at McPhee, who didn't look away from his screen but helpfully held up four fingers. Tariq nodded, understanding the taciturn porter's shorthand.

"Twenty minutes ago."

I winced. He could be anywhere by now. About to come around the corner, lying in wait next to the elevator, crouching in my corner, ready to pounce. I began to better appreciate the paranoia of citizens from dictatorial countries. In moments like these, my life was full of terror and uncertainty. Luckily, I didn't have to wait long for the axe to fall.

McPhee gave a warning grunt. "Incoming."

Tariq swivelled in his chair as we stared at McPhee. A vibration came from my pocket, but I ignored my phone, palms sweating.

A sharp tongue with a Scottish accent sounded at my back, and I jumped.

"Ms Bashir, how *nice* of you to join us this morning," Shelton oozed. "I had to check my watch to make sure it was still morning."

My heart took off aimlessly like a startled hare as Tariq

and I made eye contact. So much white showed in his eyes, it was almost comical. Even Tariq, who'd worked here for years, was still afraid of Adrian Shelton.

Plastering on my best contrite look, I turned around to face my doom, head low and hands behind my back.

Tall, freckled and as stiff as his starched suit coat was Dr Adrian Shelton. If ever a man exuded self-importance, it was he, glaring down at me through wire-rimmed spectacles. His thin lips pressed into something that was neither smile nor sneer but something in between.

Assurances to never be late again would only meet with sneers, and an excuse or justification was like putting blood in the water.

"Good morning, sir. I apologise for my tardiness."

Dr Shelton brushed aside my words with a disdainful lift of his chin. "I see you are not satisfied with simply shirking your responsibilities, but you have seen fit to enlist these men into an attempted cover-up." His accusatory eye now included the porters.

In my periphery, I watched as McPhee and Tariq shared a stricken look. It seemed Shelton had more than enough grief to go around this morning. Tariq's mouth opened to refute the accusation, but I got there first.

"You have nothing to worry about, Dr Shelton. These men remain as incorruptible as ever."

I used my hidden hand to give both men a secret thumbs up, as a little fighting spirit stirred in my chest. If Shelton wanted to rake me over the coals, that was fine. Uncle or no, I was late for work, and I'd take whatever he had for me. But going after two who were little more than bystanders was bullying, plain and simple. I had as much tolerance for bullying in the workplace as I did when I saw it in the schoolyard, and if Ian Cooper's nose was any evidence, that tolerance was zero.

"That remains to be seen." Shelton glared at the men. "For now, I still have your irresponsible behaviour to deal with."

At least Shelton seemed intent on wearing himself out on me first. That small victory gave me a dangerous boost in confidence.

"The best thing would be to send me straight downstairs, sir." I pointed to the elevator, in case he worried I'd forgotten how to get to the basement. "With any luck, I can be caught up by noon."

Shelton's watery-blue eyes glinted dangerously at my tone. I'd overstepped. It felt good momentarily, but the nasty grin spreading across his face made me queasy.

"As your supervisor, I will determine what is best, but by all means, please head to your station. I'll make sure you have no lack of opportunity to *catch up*, but first I'll need to return to the administrative offices and make a note in your file."

I refused to let him see how much that actually hurt. A demerit in my file could come back to haunt me, especially when I needed to find real work in the field. I nodded diffidently. "Will that be all, Dr Shelton?"

Shelton flapped a dismissive hand. "Run along, Ms Bashir, you're appallingly behind in your duties. Perhaps the work will give you time to clear your head for the conversation you will undoubtedly have with your Proctor."

I'd begun to go, one foot back and shoulders turning, but his words spun me around like a slap across the face. Proctor? He was really going to go to the university over this? A bad note in my file was one thing, but a call to the academic discipline was another. The museum and the uni worked in close concert, and that meant such a call could have far-reaching consequences. Depending on how grossly I was mischaracterised, I could see sanction or even expulsion from the programme.

I met Shelton's glare, daring me to say something, anything he could use against me. Only thinking of Uncle Iry kept me from giving him what he wanted and more besides.

"Very good, sir. I should get going then."

He almost seemed disappointed by my response.

I felt Tariq and McPhee's pitying eyes on me as I strode towards the elevators, but I didn't look back. I couldn't. I was trying to hold everything together. I wasn't sure if I wanted to break Shelton's nose or burst into tears.

Uncle Iry, I reminded myself. *For him. For being a family again.*

I swiped for the elevator and was granted the small mercy of not having to wait more than a few seconds for the doors to slide open. A tall, silver-haired gentleman in wire-rimmed spectacles straight out of the thirties stepped off, giving me a curious look that I ignored.

Stepping inside, I refused to look at anything but the console. The doors shut. The elevator came to life with a little jump, and I slumped against the back of the compartment. My hands tightened around the handrail, squeezing until my fingers popped and my palms ached. I released the rail with a shuddering sigh and remembered my phone.

Reflexively, I drew it out and swiped the screen on.

Message: Jackie D.

Hey darling, u still up for a nite at the Hen w/ ur besty? Pls, I NEED to c u!

A string of pictures of various mammals with imploring eyes followed the text, and despite everything I'd just gone through, I found myself smiling, just a little. I punched out a response, thankful that the museum wi-fi was among the best available. The elevator came to a halt, and the doors slid open. Stepping out, I hit reply.

Sure. I need some fun.

By the time I reached my dark little corner, a trio of animated fireworks blitzed across my screen.

Luv, that's what I'm all about!!! XOXO, C u at 8!

Jackie and I had been friends since starting uni together. If I'd learned anything about her, it was that — she'd spoken truly — fun was what she was all about. In all the best and worst ways. I wasn't sure a night out with her was what I should do, but right then, it was what I needed.

Chapter Three

The floor that comprised Collections was called the dungeon, even though it was not the lowest level of the museum. It might have been because the whole floor was perpetually dark, only little islands of light pooled at each workstation. It could also have been because anyone who was unlucky enough to work down here had the same expectations as any prisoner; going nowhere fast.

I found the light switch for my station and gave a groan as my desk was flooded with light. I had thought Dr Shelton was just being mean when he'd said I was appallingly behind in my work. Turned out he knew something I didn't.

True to form, Dr Shelton had shunted full exhibits from two departments to me. They sat in disorderly piles on stainless steel trollies, lined up like a fleet of bad news bombers. One was labelled French Revolution; Continental History, while the other stated Updates; Archives.

That was a dirty one on Shelton's part — sending me bits from Archives. The pieces from Archives weren't being considered for an exhibit and had done nothing but sit since the last time they were processed. It was a formality. It allowed the records department to feel satisfied that no one had run off with a potsherd or lead bearing. Besides being useless, they were also notorious for being hard to process. Most of the forgotten pieces in Archives had no entry in the computer system. They might even be labelled under a different classification than what was on their dusty storage containers. It meant I'd more than likely have to go through the laborious business of creating a whole new entry.

As I said, Shelton is a git.

I pulled up my stool and turned on the computer tower and monitor. The whirr of an ancient fan fought to keep the crotchety processor cool. The monitor blinked **SEARCHING FOR SIGNAL** for a moment, and the status light changed from orange to green as the system began to boot up.

That was a relief.

Sometimes, the decades-old computers we used would refuse to work at all, stalling like stubborn mules, quitting halfway up a mountain trail. If the computer's connection to the museum's network was disturbed by one of its microchips giving a geriatric cough, you could lose the entire entry and have to start over.

In a word: tedious. I'd been doing this for months, and — if this morning was any indication — I would be doing it for many months more.

After the computer had finally primed, I pulled up the Collections menu and found the Updates directory. The window soon filled with row after row of items. A quick glance had me stifling a moan of despair. Many of them bore old designations from before the latest updates to the system. As I eyed the boxes, I wondered if I would have time to slip out for my afternoon lectures with this much work ahead of me.

My father's mantra gave me the impetus to quit moping and get to work: no job was ever finished by crying about it.

Walking over to the farthest trolley, I grabbed the first box and lugged it to my desk.

Even though he was a damn fine automotive mechanic, he spent almost every day since coming to the UK in the lowest paying, most menial jobs available. Every employer assumed because of Sudan's poverty and troubled history my father's credentials were either worthless or an outright lie. For all that though, he never complained in front of me, and he always said he was happy to work any job if it fed his family.

Family was all that mattered, and so for my family or what was left of it, I processed that stack. Then the next stack and the next. Soon they would need to be rolled down to Archives for filing. The thought of being able to escape from behind my computer screen, even for fifteen minutes, gave me a fresh burst of motivation.

I was so enthused by the thought of even a short break I failed to pay attention to how crowded my station was getting.

My elbow clipped one of the last three boxes. I watched — helpless — as it skidded across the desk to teeter at the very edge. I was already moving, but not fast enough. The box hit the floor with a heavy crunch. The seal broke, and black powder exploded outwards.

An instant later, the whole floor went dark. The lack of unhappy murmurs from the other stations meant I was working through lunch and hadn't even noticed. As though to chastise me for this, my stomach gave a loud grumble.

The utter black was a shock, but a moment later, I dug my phone out of my pocket. Power fluctuations were as common down here as was the gossip in the admin office. Someone, somewhere had overtaxed the system. We were the first to feel the backlash. I sometimes wondered if the whole bloody thing was designed that way. After all, our work was the least important. On any other day, I might have sat there and waited, but I had too much to do, and now I also had a mess to clean up.

The phone light stabbed brilliantly through the dark. Several bits of grimy ceramic and metal lay across the ground, cushioned by a thin bed of dark soil. I cursed under my breath at the fragments of pottery and metal, pretty sure that 'broken' wasn't their original state.

I'd never damaged an artefact before and vaguely wondered in an unattached way if Shelton would fire me on the spot. The mess alone would drive him up a wall, without even mentioning that I'd destroyed something centuries old.

Glowering, I stalked towards the supply closet, suddenly glad for the cover of darkness. I needed to get the things cleaned-up and take it to Cataloguing. I'd ask Meredith what to do.

Meredith Janssen, a senior research assistant, was the closest thing I had to a confidante at work. We'd conversed often while I was there to pick up something from an outgoing exhibit. She'd intimated that she'd been 'dealing' with Shelton for years and sympathised. I'd never pressed beyond that, but I hoped now I had a real crisis in which she'd actually be able to help.

I scrounged up a broom and a dustpan, and I returned to my station just as the power returned.

In the glare of the overhead lights, the scope of the mess became clear, and I stood there stunned at just how much dirt covered the floor. It seemed implausible that such a small box could have held so much. With a resigned huff, I began sweeping. Fifteen minutes later, I'd returned nearly all of the dirt to the box, and I had only to collect the broken artefact — or what was left of it. I'd laid my roll of packaging tape to reseal the thing, but I wondered after I'd gotten it out if sealing it all back up was tantamount to a cover-up.

Some angrier, uglier side of me answered *who cares?* But in the end, I decided to stick with my plan. Ask Meredith.

I was about to dump the fragments back into the container when something caught my eye. Burnished lustre of metal stood out against the broken bits of pottery. The kind of metal wasn't immediately obvious, though at a glance, I guessed it was a copper alloy. A quick check of the storage label said that the box was supposed to contain early Hittite pottery — no mention of metals.

A powerful curiosity took root.

Setting the dustpan on my work table, I got down on my hands and knees. Delicately, I used a pen to shift the mess around to get a better look at the metal fragments.

It soon became clear they weren't fragments at all, but thick rings, two of them, cut through a single piece of metal so they were attached. Each had a wide band etched with cuneiform that looked more Sumerian or Akkadian than Hittite. One side of the rings was uneven, and the lighter grey of exposed metal suggested they'd been broken. If worn, the rings would entirely cover two fingers from the middle to the base knuckle. The strange half-gauntlet had faint, rippling striations. Evidence of a forging process I hadn't seen even after hours studying metallurgic techniques used by ancient cultures.

I checked the box over one more time, searching for something that defined such an exciting and unique artefact. There was nothing anywhere in or on the box that explained the two rings.

Looked like I had more than just my screw-up to discuss with Meredith.

I CALLED her name softly from the door of Cataloguing Lab D.

A short, stout woman with a mess of brown curls stepped away from a lab table where she and two other colleagues stood. She blinked owlishly from behind wide spectacles, and her face lit up with recognition.

"Ibby, I haven't seen you for donkey's years," she said kindly as she came over to the door.

Meredith was always cheerful and prone to cockney slang, even if it irritated the more uppity members of the staff, not least of all a certain supervisor. That might have been why we got on so well.

"I've missed you too. I'm not interrupting something important, am I?"

Meredith tossed a dismissive hand. "Don't think on it for a minute, dear. I'll just let those boys chase their tails for a bit." She stepped closer and lowered her voice. "Between you and me, the two of us together could do the work of three sets of these knobheads."

I covered my mouth to hide a smile. It was impossible not to like Meredith. "A true compliment if I've ever heard one." I gestured to the hallway. "Can I show you something out here?"

Meredith nodded, and together we slid out into the hallway where I'd left the trolley laden with boxes. From the top, I took the box containing the strange rings, looked up and down the hall and stole a glance over Meredith's shoulder at the knobheads. They weren't paying us any attention.

"I had an accident when the power flickered earlier," I said, keeping my voice low, "but it led me to a fascinating discovery."

Popping the box open, I took the pen I'd tucked behind my ear and reached in to hook the rings. Meredith watched wordlessly as they hung in the air before her face, glinting in the subdued light of the hallway.

"This box is labelled early Hittite pottery, but look at this. I've never seen anything like it. If these markings are Hittite, then I'm a dandelion."

Meredith produced a latex glove from her jacket pocket and took the rings, curiosity etched across her features. A few times, she used her free hand to raise her glasses to the top of her head and back down again. As she inspected them, she murmured without meeting my eyes, "Exactly what kind of accident did you have?"

Something in Meredith's tone made me uncomfortable, but I remembered how seriously she took her job, and I supposed she was just trying to be professional. I told her about Shelton dumping all the extra work on me. That had led to my crowded workstation and accidentally knocking the box off my desk, the power going out and the subsequent discovery. Meredith listened, her expression now unreadable.

"So now, I have two problems: one is what to do with the compromise in artefact storage, and second is who I should report this to? I don't trust Shelton not to turn it into an excuse to sack me."

She frowned, shook her head and took the box from me. Unceremoniously, she dropped the rings back inside and closed the box. She held it out to me at arm's length.

"Seal it and put it back in Archives with the other bits you have there." She jerked her chin towards the trolley.

Incredulous, I blinked at her. Was she really telling me to cover it up? Ignore it? Not tell anyone? Was I supposed to pretend I hadn't found new, possibly unique metallurgical evidence in some forgotten pottery fragments?

"Really?"

She nodded emphatically and pressed the box against my stomach, where my arms reflexively came up to take it. "That's exactly what I'm telling you to do."

"But … why?"

My mind was racing. I mentally reviewed every word I'd said, everything I'd done, but none of it added up to this. Feelings of betrayal began to creep up my spine. I had thought I could trust her to help me out, not to encourage me to bury the strange thing. Wasn't that the worst choice? The rings wouldn't see the light of day again for decades. It would eventually become someone else's find, but in the meantime, its secrets would remain hidden, its story undiscovered.

I realised then Meredith didn't see it as a *find* but as a *problem*.

"Short answer," she replied, "is that you've had a spell o' bad cheese, love."

"I don't get what that has to do with … "

Meredith shook her head abruptly, her mouth opening to say something before it closed again, and she glanced back over her shoulder into the lab. She took my arm and led me a short distance down the hall, which had a window that offered a view of Cataloguing Lab D. Her two colleagues appeared to be engaged in an argument over an artefact on the table. Meredith knocked her head towards them.

"Do you want to be in here someday, Ibby?"

"You know I do." My hopes and ambitions extended well beyond the Cataloguing Lab, but that was beside the point of what she was insinuating. She had my attention.

"Labs like these exist because museums pay for them, and like any institution, they don't take kindly to having their mistakes exposed. No one likes their dirty knickers on display. You follow?"

I did, and I nodded around the lump of unease that was forming in my throat.

"Good girl. See, you bring this up to Shelton or one of the other bigwigs, and it will look like we've got a major muck up in Collections. Remember some of those artefacts are on loan from other museums or are even of ... disputable provenance. Embarrassments galore, then accusations and the great bloody witch hunt. Who do you think serves as the perfect scapegoat?"

I began to feel very alone. It seemed terribly unfair, worse than unfair; it seemed dishonest and cowardly. I fought to keep my voice from breaking. "But what if this is the discovery of a lifetime? What if this is the revelation that leads to a hundred more?"

Meredith looked me in the eye, seeming ten years older and very sad. "Then it is up to somebody else to find out." At my stricken look, she offered me a bone. "Maybe you can rediscover it when you're not at bottom of the pile. For you, right here, right now," she jabbed at the box in my arms, "that little find is a landmine."

I looked down at it, blinking back my disappointment. My hands trembled, and I thought I could hear bits rattling about inside, the metallic clink of the rings against the ceramics seemed to taunt me. Or were they calling to me?

Meredith reached out and steadied my hands. I met

her eyes and saw they were filled with pity. "That's my advice, love. I know you'll do what's for the best."

Then she was gone, and I was left standing there with the landmine.

PUSHING THE TROLLEY TOWARDS ARCHIVES, I was thankful that besides the odd porter on patrol, hardly anyone came here. Otherwise, my foot-dragging pace might have drawn some attention.

The nefarious little box sat on top of the stack, reminding me I hadn't made up my mind to follow Meredith's advice. People travelled to the far corners of the earth, hoping for a discovery like this. A good number of them never found anything. When one literally fell on the floor in front of me, could I cover it up and pretend that nothing had happened?

I was approaching a corner when I heard the click of hard soles on the floor. My heart skipped a beat. The porters and most of the staff all wore soft shoes to avoid excessive noise on the hard floors. But Dr Shelton wore loud-soled shoes. I often thought he did it on purpose to call attention to himself. The steps were coming my way. Any second now, he'd round the bend.

On impulse, I snatched up the box and slipped it into my bag. The movement was so simple and smooth I realised I had made up my mind after all. I just hadn't admitted it. Putting my weight behind the trolley, I did my best to appear as diligent and innocuous as possible.

Only it wasn't Dr Shelton who came around the corner.

He was a tall gentleman in a tweed sport coat, whose feathered silver hair did an admirable job of covering his thinning hairline. Salt and pepper stubble on his cheeks seemed a little out of place, considering how traditionally well-dressed he was.

I didn't recognise him at all.

That alone was notable, given we were in a part of the museum that was only for staff; further, I was familiar with everyone from both the day and evening shifts. It was not as though members of the public made tours down to Archives on a whim. This unfamiliarity, paired with how he didn't appear to notice me and my trolley as he walked past, made things downright bizarre.

"Can I help you?" I asked, halting the trolley and casting my eye over him for an ID badge. Perhaps he was a new professor at the university.

The man stopped dead in his tracks and turned to regard me. His dark eyes were wide behind his horn-rimmed spectacles. He just stared.

"Sir?" I prompted when he made no reply.

Old instincts kicked in, reminding me I was on a nearly abandoned floor of the museum with some strange, staring man I didn't know. Putting the trolley squarely between us, I gathered up the straps of my bag. Hidden artefact or no, I'd swing it right into those spectacles if he stepped out of line.

His eyewear sparked something in my memory. I *had* seen him before, coming off the elevator after my encounter with Shelton this morning. The look he'd given me then was not dissimilar to the one he wore now. I relaxed. In all likelihood, I was dealing with a visiting scholar — one of the more socially awkward academics. It wouldn't be the first time I'd had to deal with some gawky bookworm who struggled to communicate with members of his own species, particularly those of the opposite sex. Training and working in a specialised field attracted eccentric personalities. While some were easier to get along with than others, a smile and patience went a long way with most.

I put on my gentlest smile. "Are you lost?"

He started at my question, one hand coming up to his mouth. Then with what seemed like an incredible effort, he finally spoke, "S-s-so sor-ry, madame. I'm-m feeling a touch-ch under the w-weather."

He seemed healthy enough to me, maybe a little thin. "I'm sorry to hear that."

His gaze wandered to the stacked trolley between us where it lingered on each box before meandering back to me. When he spoke this time, the words seemed to come easier.

"Excuse me, I'm being rude. I'm Professor James Lowe, Mesopotamian Studies. You are headed down to Archives, Miss …?"

"Ibby Bashir, and yes, but if you need something, I'd be happy to be of assistance."

He glanced at the trolley again, probing and sifting. I had just begun to wonder if the man was senile or possibly intoxicated, when his gaze snapped back to me.

"I'll be fine, thank you. Carry on. I imagine you have a schedule to keep."

He stepped to the side and waved me by.

I steered the trolley past him with a word of thanks and farewell. He mumbled something I couldn't quite make out, and I heard his hard soles setting off down the hallway again as I rounded the corner.

I was shaking my head at the bizarre incident when what he'd said about schedules sank in. I snatched out my phone to check the time.

"Bollocks!" I snarled and threw myself against the trolley.

The drama of the morning had driven all other thoughts from my mind. Shelton's recent threats echoed in my memory as I realised I simply had to be at my first lecture on time. I could not afford to be late, and the class started in ten minutes!

Chapter Four

I made it to each of my lectures, though I did have to admit defeat and creep into the first one nearly ten minutes late. The first one was the largest and held in a big auditorium with poor lighting, especially when it was raining. Which — during the London winter — meant often. I was thankful for that.

For all the effort I'd exerted to get to my lectures, I didn't learn a thing. I sat there the entire time keenly aware of the artefact sitting in my bag. The *stolen* artefact.

I felt ill thinking about it.

I hadn't intended to steal it. The whole thing just sort of happened. Hiding it in my bag when I thought Shelton was coming turned into forgetting it was there while racing to get to my lectures, which turned into yanking open my bag to get a pad for notes and realising that I'd committed a crime. If I hadn't seen a few classmates noticing my flabbergasted expression, I would have continued to sit there, blinking into my bag in horror. I grabbed the pad, closed my bag, faced the front and scribbled notes about nothing.

It was awful. I almost lost my nerve altogether. When

moving between lecture halls, I collided with a young woman in the corridor. The box gave a rattle, and I looked down to see the clasp was undone. Squeaking out an apology, I frantically ducked into the nearest loo while trying to refasten the bag. Shutting myself in a stall, I closed the bag and sat on the toilet lid to catch my breath. I gulped in air and realised I was sweating … sweating and talking to myself under my breath.

"This is mad. I'm mad. It's a nightmare. I just need to take it back. Take it back and listen to Meredith."

"Everything all right in there, dear?" The voice was husky and slightly accented.

I froze, not daring to breathe. I hoped she was talking to someone else.

Two laboured heartbeats later, there came a soft rap on the stall door and the question was repeated. This was not my day. Scrambling, I flushed and called out over the rushing water.

"Out in a minute!"

I checked the bag was firmly shut and opened the stall door.

A young woman I'd run into in the hallway stood a respectful distance away, but was clearly waiting for me. Of medium height and build, she was a striking woman with full lips and a smooth, rich complexion. Her skin had dark, deep tones close to my own, but her features and hair were not African or Asiatic. Dark, expressive eyes filled with concern locked on mine.

"I don't usually follow people into the loo," she said, "but you took off like a shot, looking in a bad way. I just wanted to make certain you were all right. You seem … distressed."

"I'm fine." The words came out in a waspish snap I hadn't intended. I moved past her to the sinks. In the bathroom mirror she watched me, studying my face. I looked into the mirror and frowned. I looked like a wretch. No wonder she'd pursued me. Sweat beaded on my forehead and upper lip. My clothes were dishevelled, and the muscles in my arms trembled, making my hands shake.

I took a breath and willed my brain to think of something to say. It would be easy to put the woman off by being rude, but she didn't deserve that.

Ibby. My father's voice rose in my mind with gentle admonition. *Just because the world is ugly, this is no excuse to make things worse. Make it better by being better.*

I ran my hands under the water, snatched a paper towel, then turned to face the good Samaritan as I dried my hands. "I'm sorry, I didn't mean to snap. I am having a rough day. I'm afraid there is no easy answer for pushy bosses and missing my family."

The woman nodded, her eyes sage in a way at odds with her youthful face. "I understand. You're right, there are rarely easy answers for such things."

I pitched the towel into the rubbish bin and faced her with a self-conscious grin I didn't have to fake. "I'm sorry for smashing into you like that. Are you a student here?"

She appeared to be the right age but wasn't carrying any of the usual paraphernalia — bags, books or various electronics. She had dark slacks, a muted red top, dark roman sandals and that was it, not even a purse.

"I'm considering it. Still trying to see where I fit in best. I'm Daria, by the way. Daria Tehom, but most just call me Dary."

She extended a hand, and I took it, hoping she didn't mind that mine was still damp.

"I'm Ibby."

Dary smiled as her phone buzzed from her pocket,

prompting an apologetic look as she fetched it, scanned the screen and tucked it away again.

"Well, it seems the dean I was waiting for is available now. It's been a pleasure, Ibby. I hope things turn out all right. Chin up. Maybe we can swap stories over a cuppa sometime. If I stick around."

I nodded and muttered something vague but sincere about that being nice. She'd reminded me that I had to be somewhere as well.

I followed her out of the loo, stepping on the back of her shoe. I apologised profusely as I hefted my bag onto my shoulder. As soon as I was clear of the door, I rushed down the hall again.

THE REST of my afternoon and early evening was uneventful but just as unproductive. Try as I might, I couldn't forget I was toting stolen antiquities.

I made up my mind to take the box back after I met with my adviser. That would mean I wouldn't get to go home before going to meet Jackie, but at least I could be done with the whole debacle. A plan firmly in mind, I felt a little better as I headed to the café where my adviser and I usually met.

Professor Yun Schottelkirk was something of a rock star in the small pond that was the university archaeology department. A second-generation Chinese immigrant with degrees in both archaeology and geology, she'd pioneered a new technique for excavating in mountainous regions in her younger days. Now, with more silver than black in her hair, she'd settled into teaching and raising a family when she wasn't being called out to lecture or consult.

As I said, rock star.

With me, she was down-to-earth and gracious, even going so far as to insist on paying for my snacks at the café. It took a month of cajoling before I took her up on anything more than a cup of tea and biscuits. Now I looked forward to consuming a meal without counting the value of what I was eating down to the pence.

"It's good for students to be poor while in school," Professor Schottelkirk had once said confidently. "Knocks some of the arrogance out of them. But, a treat every once and a while won't spoil that."

After the day's antics, which had not included anything other than my morning coffee, I was ready for a sandwich. When a mound of roast beef on flatbread was set before me, I attacked it with vigour. My adviser was kind enough to do the bulk of the talking, congratulating me on my good marks on an exam and then talking through my schedule for the coming semester. It wasn't until I was picking at the crumbs of my meal that I remembered Shelton's promise to call the Proctor. Since she hadn't said anything so far, Shelton hadn't done it yet or Schottelkirk hadn't gotten the news yet. I didn't think he was going to forget or change his mind. That man would never pass up a chance to grind someone beneath his heel, even by proxy.

When we were finished discussing my education, I told Professor Schottelkirk about the morning's exchange with Shelton. When she asked why I was so late, I explained I'd been talking with my uncle in the early hours of the morning. She was aware of my family situation and would ask after Uncle Irshad sometimes.

Schottelkirk settled back into her chair and sipped her tea thoughtfully. I sat quietly, trying not to think about how the sandwich felt as though it was slowly inflating inside my belly.

She put down her cup abruptly. "Shelton is a prat," she declared. "He is a prat and a bully, and if he doesn't watch himself, he's going to learn what happens to those who become more trouble than they're worth."

I liked this line of thinking, though I couldn't help wondering if Schottelkirk's prophesying equated to anything useful. Shelton's future sacking wouldn't matter much if I had already been shown the door.

"I'm glad you brought this to me, Ibby," she patted my hand. "I will see the Proctor myself and nip this nonsense in the bud. You need to keep up a good show at work, nose clean and all that, and obviously, don't be late again. But leave the rest to me."

She had this way of saying things that incited confidence, and I couldn't keep from smiling. Maybe, it was going to be all right.

I put a hand on my bag and was on the verge of bringing up my discovery when I stopped short. She'd already declared she'd go to bat for me once. Did I really want to ask more of her?

"Thank you, Professor," I said instead, sitting back in my chair. "I appreciate that so much."

With our meeting adjourned, I headed back to the museum. The box was going into Archives, and I was going to forget I ever found anything in the first place.

MARCUS, the night-time porter, was surprised when I trotted in. He made an observation about 'burning the candle at both ends' as I swiped in.

Marcus was the youngest of the porters who provided surveillance for the museum and worked only nights. I hardly ever saw him. He was a competitive bodybuilder in his spare time and looked the part, his muscular frame straining at the confines of his uniform. His physique had inspired unofficial complaints from several female museum employees that he didn't work during the daytime, offering an improvement from the dumpy figures of Tariq and McPhee or even the grizzled Eddy. I was indifferent. Marcus was nice to look at, sure. But I had more pressing things on my mind.

That, and Jackie had enough romantic drama for the two of us.

Thinking of Jackie, I needed to let her know I might be late. The Hen — Jackie's favourite haunt — was on the north edge of Chelsea, and the tube would be mad with commuters at this time.

I took out my phone as I journeyed the quiet halls and tapped out a text.

Jackie's replies came in rapid succession.

U better not stand me up!

I need to see u

Things must be shared!

That last text was Jackie's way of saying she had a new gent, though calling them 'gents' was giving them more credit than any so far deserved. As long as I'd known her, Jackie's type included cads and codependent arseholes. I was slightly less excited about seeing her as I rode the elevator down to Archives.

When I arrived, I realised it would seem odd that I was filing a single item during the hours I usually didn't work. I might have been acting paranoid, but recalling what Schottelkirk said had me muttering and thumbing the elevator back up to Collections, without leaving the box.

Nose clean and all that.

There were a few odd containers left for Archives so I set to work on those. I could make it look like I was stopping by to finish up the odd bit of the extra work Shelton had given me. It was a good thing I'd told Jackie I was going to be late.

I'd made it through all but two boxes when the door opened. Hard-heeled shoes clopped across the floor, coming my way. Shelton coming to check on me? Nerves fluttered in my belly as I looked at the bag sitting at my feet, the box still within.

Should I take it out and throw it onto the stack? What if he spotted me taking it out? What if he asked to search my bag? I shook my head like a confused puppy. Why would he search my bag?

The debate was — thankfully — unnecessary. The same silver-haired gentleman from earlier strode up the stacks, coming my way.

A prickle that something was off about this man lifted my arm hair. My gaze remained on him as he leisurely strolled towards my little island of light amidst the dim sea.

Three times in one day, this strange man had crossed my path. Why? This couldn't be an accident.

Professor Lowe said just before stepping into the direct light of my workstation. "Good evening, madame."

"Evening," I replied, aiming for relaxed and sounding robotic instead. "Feeling better, sir?"

What was he doing down here? Again? Still? Old instincts kicked in from the rougher years of living in public housing, and I began to case out my exits.

My workstation was located almost exactly in the middle of the Collections floor, which meant I was equidistant from the two doorways leading to the stairs at one end and the elevators at the other. If things went funny, I could fake a rush towards one door and then double back between the rows to reach the other side. I could also pull storage containers down behind me to slow him down. If he caught me, I could use a pen … or scissors …

My fingers crept casually towards the shears sitting at the corner of my desk.

He stepped to the workstation table opposite me and looked back the way he'd come.

"Much better, thank you. My, it is dreary down here. Different from when I was on staff. Would it kill them to put some light and colour into the place?"

I blinked in surprise. "You worked here, Professor?" I stopped reaching for the scissors.

His frown at the decor turned into a kindly, almost paternal grin as his eyes found mine.

"Once upon a time. I was a professor of the university of course, but I also served as a consultant for the museum. Some of the most important work I ever did was in this building. Which brings me to why I'm here." He suddenly looked uncomfortable and took on the halting stutter he'd had before. He adjusted his spectacles and rocked back on his heels. "It is rather e-embarrassing. I was here v-visiting an old colleague and r-remembered that some time ago, a-a long time ago, I eh … misplaced an item."

I stared at him as he lapsed into silence. I was now more curious than suspicious but unsure if he was done talking. I prompted him. "What did you misplace, sir? Or maybe, where do you think you misplaced this thing?"

He started, his face twisting almost into an expression of pain. I began to wonder if the old fellow was senile, but his gaze sharpened, his stare intensely fearful. He didn't stammer now, but his next words came out in a hurried rush. "Something mixed in with bits of Assyrian pott - " He blinked. Then, suddenly: "No, it was Hittite! Hittite pottery. An artefact, but not something which belongs to the museum or the university. Something else. Something very important."

The specific mention of Hittite pottery made my blood run cold and inspired a hundred terrifying thoughts, none of them fully formed before the next one bubbled up. I gaped at him, not sure what to say.

Fortunately, Professor Lowe took my shocked silence as a response to bad manners rather than a guilty conscience.

"I'm terribly sorry," he muttered, pale face flushing. "That was very abrupt of me. It is just … very important to me and not me alone."

I nodded, feigning understanding because I still had no idea what to say. It seemed impossible this retired professor would now come looking for his long-lost treasure. Why today? The day I not only found it but also the day my future and that of my uncle hung in the balance. If Lowe learned I'd taken artefacts out of the museum, I would be just as finished as if Shelton had found out.

Oblivious to my mental panic, he continued, "You haven't, perhaps, had such a collection come across your desk?"

I gave him a frozen smile as my mind scampered to and fro. If I held off on admitting it now and 'made the discovery' tomorrow, no one would be the wiser. This strange old man would get what he wanted, I would be safe and the pressure of handling my discovery would be off.

"I haven't, but I'll look into it tomorrow, Professor," I replied. "I promise. But right now, I'm late to meet a friend."

Lowe straightened and adjusted his jacket. I was reminded that he had no ID badge, not even a visitor pass.

The prickling fingers along my spine returned. Even if he was an old warhorse of the museum, no one was allowed to walk around without some sort of identification.

Did I want to call him out on it? While I was alone? And if he kept the pass in his pocket or something, would he be offended?

"It is rather late, isn't it?" he observed.

"Yes, I was just on my way out," I remarked. "Professor, if you wouldn't mind walking me out? I would appreciate the company." Let Marcus see what could be made of this gentleman.

He straightened his sport coat again. "Certainly. It would be a pleasure."

I smiled as daintily as I could, keyed my station to power off and picked up my bag.

WE WERE JUST EXITING the elevator to the lobby when Lowe snapped his fingers and pressed them to his lips.

"Dash it all! I've just remembered I've some business to attend to before I leave tonight."

A glance showed Marcus at the security desk, his broad back to us and head bowed. Probably on his phone. I frowned. So helpful.

"If you find anything at all, please stop by the British Museum Station. Oh, but you will need a map. Wait right here. I'll fetch you one."

I blinked. British Museum Station? He must have meant Tottenham Court Road. And what map? I had an app for the London Underground. Who used maps anymore? Even antiquated professors knew how to use travel apps these days. I glared at the back of Marcus's head, willing him to turn around.

But Lowe had already left my side, passing between the glass double doors towards the administrative wing. A heartbeat more, and he was out of sight.

I stomped over to Marcus. “Fat lot of good you are,” I snapped. One look at his face made me regret the outburst instantly.

Marcus managed to look embarrassed, afraid and shocked all at once, the expression all the more absurd for sitting atop his thickly muscled shoulders. He slapped his phone down like it was too hot to touch, and blinked at me like a beat dog.

“What happened?”

I softened my voice. “There’s a man walking around without an ID badge or visitor pass or anything. Says he’s a retired professor. He was down in Collections, looking for something.”

Markus frowned, one hand absently picking up the clipboard holding the visitor’s log. “What was he looking for?”

“Shouldn’t your question be: where is he now? Seriously, Marcus.” I’d stung him again, and again I felt regret. It was little consolation telling myself I was right. “I’m sorry,” I said as Marcus’s mouth began to open. “I’m a little rattled.”

A fierce light came into Marcus’s eyes then, fiery and righteous. “Did he hurt you?”

Before I could answer, Marcus was on his feet, every muscle taut, an effect all the more dramatic for the number of them … muscles, I mean. He looked like a king cobra, its hood wide and spitting fiercely.

“N-no, no he didn’t,” I stammered, caught off guard. “But I ran into him three times today. He’s up to something.”

Marcus scooped up his radio and a flashlight, though why he needed the latter when all the lights were still on, I couldn’t guess.

“Which way did he go?” Marcus’s voice was low and

serious. Something resembling pity flashed through my mind for Lowe.

"Admin." I knocked my head towards the glass doors.

That was all Marcus needed. He made a beeline for the glass doors, flicking a switch on his radio. "Charlie, I have an intruder who's been harassing museum staff," the porter growled. "He's been spotted heading into the administrative offices. I'm in pursuit."

Charlie squawked through the radio grille, "Pursuit? Steady on there, hotshot!"

I lost the rest of the conversation as Marcus vanished through the double doors.

I stood there dumbly for a moment longer, wondering just how big a mess I'd made now, and then I checked the time on my phone.

Map or no, if I hurried, I wouldn't be too late to meet Jackie.

Chapter Five

Established while Chelsea was still known as the haunt of great intellectuals and artists, The Hen and Bishop was designed for quiet drinks and friendly, intelligent conversation. I couldn't speak to the quality of conversations within its walls these days, but it was always what I hoped for as I strolled down Elystan Street.

Every month, The Hen ran a special on a different kind of liquor to bring the partiers in. That was the only way that Jackie, who loved clubs, dancing and all things bedazzled and glamorous, had discovered this spot. Since that one drunken night, she'd decided she liked it. So, she commenced a weekly ritual.

The street side tables were empty except for a couple talking loudly to each other over a beer. They looked to be having a good time, but I was glad they were outside. Obnoxious voices would have grated on my frazzled nerves.

The doorman, a craggy-faced fellow named Harris, knew me. With a courteous nod, he hooked a thumb over his shoulder. Harris's voice was like wood smoke and old scotch, rough but not unkind. "Jackie's in the back. Brace yourself. She's pretty excited about the flavour of the week."

"Thanks, Harry." I gave him a peck on the cheek that made his grey moustache twitch.

Ducking inside, I was greeted by a warm interior with exposed beams, soft amber lighting and the strains of a Leonard Cohen song. A set of roped-off stairs led to a second level. To the left was the common room from where the piano playing came, as well as the low-level hum of conversation. Woolshott, the publican — who everyone called Woolsey — spotted me from the bar as I came in. He gave a cheery wave and pointed to my right. I nodded and mouthed my thanks.

The back room was smaller with only a single row of wooden booths along the wall. Two sets of antique double doors stood propped open to a small cobbled yard that had a few tables and chairs.

Jackie had chosen a booth in the back corner. Her face was highlighted by the stark glare of her phone. She looked wan and tired. But when she heard my footsteps, she looked up with the brilliant smile I loved. Jackie was gorgeous, and being her friend — her 'responsible' friend — wasn't easy sometimes.

"I thought you'd never get here!" She leapt from her seat and threw her arms around me.

She was on the tall side with a knockout figure that stood in adamant defiance of her eating habits and occasional binge drinking. Pouty lips, chocolatey-brown eyes and immaculate waves of dark hair, Jackie turned heads wherever she went and with whatever she wore. She laughed easily and warmly, could make anyone feel special and had a charming mischievous streak.

"You say 'things must be shared.' I come running." I

released her and slid into the booth. "That's how this works. Don't you know?" I pointed to her, then myself and back again in rapid succession with both hands.

Jackie laughed. Catching the attention of a passing waiter, she asked for two glasses and a bottle of wine, before scooping her phone back up.

"Oh, and don't I just have things to share," she giggled.

I braced myself. We'd gone through this often enough, as the code implied, and each time I dreaded this part the most. She would show me her new love interest or as she called them, *mon chou*, which was a French pastry or a candy or something. They were invariably good looking, invariably rich, or at least lived like it and invariably ended up being cads of one sort or another.

Jackie looked up from her phone, eyes twinkling, and she pressed the screen against her chest. "Ready?" She caught that pouty lower lip between her teeth in anticipation.

It was like a child asking you to watch them do something you knew was going to end badly. Nothing you could say was going to stop them, and you didn't want to crush their spirit, but you also didn't want to deal with the wreckage afterwards.

I nodded, wishing the wine was here already.

"Isn't he just delicious?"

I closed one eye and made a show of peeking as she turned the screen to face me. Catching a glimpse, both eyes popped open and I stared openly. "Good heavens."

"Right?"

The young man on the screen was a wild motorcycle ride along a rugged coast. He was a warm bear hug in front of a crackling fire and big happy shrieks on the wildest ride at the fair. Handsome didn't cover it. Dark but not unruly brows, skin that was no stranger to the sun, and a way of holding his head on sculpted shoulders that seemed a perpetual, careless shrug. It looked as though he was trying too hard, posing too much, in what he thought was an edgy half-grin, but it could have just been the picture.

"His name is Dillon Sark," she went on, gazing dreamily at the phone. "We hit it off at that party you couldn't make it to last weekend."

Yeah, I'd been 'sick.'

Handsome, carefree and just enough edge to whet a girl's imagination. He had 'Jackie's type' stamped on his wrinkle-free forehead.

"He's hot." I didn't know what else to say.

"Yes … but," she started as her eyes flashed up and down again. "Is that all you're going to say?" Her voice turned soft, vulnerable.

"Jackie, what do you want me to say?" I pleaded. "I don't even know the bloke."

Jackie stared tenderly at the picture. "You just sound so … so, unenthusiastic. Almost like you're disappointed."

Tired and stressed as I was, I felt for my friend. Despite her high-flying lifestyle, I was one of the few people Jackie actually felt close to. She partied with lots of people, but she 'trusted' me.

"Jackie," I began emphatically to get her attention. "If you say he is lovely, then I hope to God he is. I just don't want to see you hurt like all those other times."

"What do you mean 'all those other times'?"

The wine arrived and not a moment too soon. Jackie measured us out two healthy glasses. Jackie's would be gone in two swallows. Sigh. Responsibility.

"I'm just saying," I explained gently, "that when you are as beautiful and fun as you are, men are drawn to you.

Many of them don't have the most honourable of intentions."

"I don't want them to be too honourable." Jackie rolled her eyes and giggled at the stricken expression on my face. "Jokes, Ibby. Just a joke."

"Joke or not, you remember Eric, don't you?"

Jackie stared at me for a second, looking like she was searching her memory, then rolled her eyes again. "I try not to."

"What about Yusef?"

This time Jackie winced and tried to hide behind her nearly empty wine glass, cheeks flushing. "Eh, let's not."

I should have stopped there, but I was on a roll and felt a powerful sense of vindication in taking a trip down the gallery of rogues and aborted romances. "Sammy? Carlo?"

Jackie gave a little groan of despair and crossed her hands in front of her face. "Mercy, please!" She half-whined, half-laughed. "You're going to make me cry."

She was playing it down, but we both knew the words were hitting close to home. As I watched Jackie pour herself another glass of wine, I cursed myself for letting fatigued irritation sharpen my tongue. I reached across the table and took her hand. She stopped pouring and looked at me.

"Jackie, I'm sorry," I said, utter sincerity making my voice shake a little. "I just want you to be with someone who treats you well and who you can fall in love with. Someone you can trust. That's all. I get my guard up because I want to protect you."

Jackie put the bottle down, gazing at me in surprise at the sudden show of seriousness.

"I'm sure he's fantastic," I affirmed before things got too uncomfortable. "I'm just being a grouse because my day went completely pear-shaped."

Concern creased her flawless brow as her dark eyes went wide. "What happened?"

This is why I loved this mess of a girl. At a word, she would be quids in to hear my problems.

"Was it that brute, Shelton?" Jackie was well aware of my boss-zilla.

"Nothing too terrible." I took a sip of wine, which I didn't taste. "I don't want to whinge."

"Come off it, Ibby, tell me." Jackie leaned in with interest. "If not for your own sake, then for mine."

"What do you mean?"

Jackie rested a hand tenderly on her phone. "Dillon is a poli-sci student, but he's finding politics a bit crass."

I resisted the urge to take a much larger gulp of wine. Dillon thought politics was crass. Poor baby.

"He's been talking about switching to archaeology," she continued. "I told him about your run-ins with that nasty wanker, Shelton, and encouraged him not to, at least not at our uni. Anything more you can tell me is another opportunity to steer him clear."

I'm not sure I appreciated Jackie using me as a lesson in why to avoid a field I loved, despite everything, but I wouldn't wish Shelton on anyone.

"Well, for such a noble cause …" I began, taking another drink.

I LEFT The Hen later than I should have.

I couldn't tell Jackie 'everything,' especially if she planned to tell Dillon. The business with me discovering and then accidentally absconding with the artefact, was glossed over with, "I thought I found something important, but my boss would just use it to crush me." From there, I moved into the weirdness with Professor Lowe, being late for my lectures and running into potential-student, Daria.

Jackie was a great listener, commiserating and crying out in outrage at all the right moments. Even while keeping some things from her, I felt lighter, less stressed.

The tube ride was quiet, almost restful. The swaying hum of the subway almost lulled me to sleep, so my feet were dragging on the walk back to my apartment. The streets were almost bare, and the night was humid. I found myself savouring the cool night breeze as I mulled things over.

Tomorrow, I would put the artefact back along with the last bit of Archive filings, getting rid of that headache for good. Then I was going to trust that by doing my job and taking Meredith's and Professor Schottelkirk's advice, I would survive the immediate future. Uncle Iry was going to be okay, because he was skilled and the hardest worker I knew. Even a man-eater like *Greater Nile* would see him as an asset worth protecting.

There. Comforted by the gentle English night, everything was going to be okay.

A sharp, high scream cut through the air. The hair at the nape of my neck bristled, and goose bumps swept my arms. Hissed curses followed by a wounded grunt brought the uglier memories of my younger days surging to the fore like a cold tsunami.

I froze, sweeping the dark corners. A knot of people stood in the doorway of an apartment complex just ahead. The lights in the entryway were not working or had been smashed out. All I could see were the shapes of people grappling.

I looked up and down the street, where I'd seen other pedestrians only moments before. Gone. I was the only other person in the alley. I scrambled for my phone, intending to call the police, but as my fingers fumbled, I caught the glint of a knife. Another scream pealed through the air, a woman's voice, fraught with panic.

The knife looked like a meat-cleaver or maybe a garden machete. Either way the victim's life could be measured in seconds.

"Hey!" I screamed advancing forwards, hefting my bag like a bludgeon. "Get off her!"

If either heard me, they didn't act like it. The knife-wielder reared back for a strike.

"Fuzz!" I screamed. "Coppers are on the way, you bastards!"

Both figures whirled, the one with the ugly knife taking a step towards me. His partner kept a hand on the struggling woman. Both looked young, mean and wild. A better view of their faces dissolved any confidence the threat of police would scare them off.

The knife-wielder took another step, pointing the knife at me menacingly. "Rat us out, did you?"

The steel flashed in the moonlight, and I was struck by how close I'd gotten and how very big and sharp the blade was.

I tried for a forceful reply, but my voice sounded weak and small. "They're coming. Get out of here before you and your mate get in serious trouble."

He gave me a snarling, gap-toothed grin. "Only one in serious trouble here is you, little rat." His face was positively demonic in the twilight of the street.

My heart began a full-on sprint.

His partner continued to struggle with the woman. She thrashed against him, trying to say something through the hand he had clamped over her mouth. His eyes widened and took on the cast of fear.

"Let's beat it," he said, hissing the words. "They ain't worth it."

The knife-wielder snarled and took a step closer to me. I hefted my bag and shook it threateningly. Not much of a weapon, but what else did I have?

"Donnie," the other called. "'Come on' - ufff!"

The struggling woman drove her knee into her captor's belly and twisted out of his grip. He wheezed a string of curses and groped at her, but she was up and swinging the door open, slipping inside. His fingers jammed against the door as she slammed it. The sound of a bolt clicking into place made me give a whoop of triumph.

Something blurred across my vision, and I realised with a scream - of fear this time - that the knife was coming towards my face!

I lurched back, arms windmilling. The edge of a blade flashed close enough to feel the wind of it. I scrambled backwards as Donnie's other hand reached out like a claw to grab at my jacket. If he got a hold of me, I was as good as dead.

I dodged his lunging grab twice, and then he made to ram the blade into my chest. My feet tangled, and I nearly stumbled, just managing to avoid the first thrust, but the second was coming. I lifted my bag like a shield and winced, preparing for the blow.

The blade and bag met with a queer clang, the blade veering wide. My attacker staggered after the spoiled stab as though he was being dragged, losing his footing, his free hand pinwheeling. I leapt out of the way as he flew past me, towards the unforgiving bitumen.

This jump put me right in the path of the other attacker.

He smacked into me with enough force to rattle my

teeth, and I spun to the ground. For an instant, lying on the concrete, I saw the mugger looking down at me with bulging, bloodshot eyes, and I thought *I'm dead.* Then to my surprise and relief, he stumbled past me to haul his friend to his feet.

The one with the knife looked as dazed as I felt and held up his weapon for inspection. I must have hit my head when I fell because it looked like there was nothing but a handle in his grip.

He shook the neutered handle at his friend. "What the bloody h-"

"Shut up and let's go!" The other grabbed him by the collar and began to drag. "Come on!"

The now blade-less mugger gave me a venomous glare, and he shoved the useless hilt into his pocket before turning to run. I could hear the slap of their trainers on the pavement, long after I'd lost sight of them.

The street went quiet once again. The nightmare was over.

I sat down on the street, panting and processing. I shivered as an icy sweat broke out all over my body. Drawing my knees towards my chest, I wrapped my trembling arms around my shins as my mind conjured a rapid string of memories. The woman's scream, the flash of the knife, that strange clang. The jarring impact, the empty hilt. It played over and over until my chest was tight and my breath was coming in gasps. A small sob escaped, but little by little, the grip of fear released. My breathing slowed, and the memories stopped chasing one another like ponies on a merry-go-round.

I'd nearly died, truly, but since I was in fact still alive, I couldn't just keep sitting on the street. My arse was damp.

Climbing unsteadily to my feet, I swayed for a moment or two, looking around. The street was abandoned now. Even the buildings seemed vacant. Most of their windows were black. There was no sign of the woman. The door she'd disappeared into was shut up tight.

I expected the police to arrive, but then remembered I'd made the threat without actually having made the call. I'd been too panicked. Unless the woman I'd saved had made the call, I was standing around for nothing. Heaving a sigh, I dug for my phone, thankful to find it undamaged by my fall, and I began to dial 999 for emergency services.

I reached down for my bag and spotted something shiny poking from the side. I'd just thumbed in 999 when I turned the bag over and stared at a coil of metal jutting from my bag. It pierced through the exterior of the tough nylon and seemed stuck fast. My thumb hovered over send as I stared at the oddity. Tugging on the corkscrew of steel, I watched in fascination as the corner of the artefact box protruded through the gash in my bag, stuck fast to the knife.

I stared stupidly at this strange sight until I realised I still hadn't dialled. I cleared the 999 and hurried down the street towards my flat.

Suddenly I was desperate not to be around if any police did show up. The last thing I needed was a bobby asking what was jutting out of my bag.

Oh nothing, officer. Just something I stole from the museum where I work.

Chapter Six

Back in my tiny, alley-side flat I sat on my only stool, hunkered over my bag.

One hand wrapped in a doubled over dish rag, the other holding the artefact box, I tried to prise the spiral of metal free. I managed to rip the hole in my bag wider and rattle some bits in the box around, but nothing else. My frustrated efforts were delicate work because — as one bandage already proved — the coiled blade was wickedly sharp.

With a grunt of frustration, I dropped it all onto the countertop and pressed both hands to my temples. I needed to get this coil away from the box if I was going to file it tomorrow with the rest. A cut, even a hole in the box, would be shrugged off as part of the normal wear and tear, and I could get a new one if need be. A warped knife? Not so much.

I tried once more, to no avail. It was stuck fast, and I couldn't even get it out of my sack without ripping a larger hole in my bag.

At my wits end, I fished out a plastic food storage

container and emptied the contents of the artefact box into it. I would swipe a new one when I got to work. It was riskier, because all boxes were dealt out when an old or damaged one was being disposed of or when we got new artefacts, but I didn't have much of a choice. I would figure out how to salvage my bag after I returned the pilfered museum property.

It was awkward opening and emptying the box while it was still inside my bag. When I heard the bigger pieces fall into their temporary home, I drew them out for inspection. Inside the food container was a good deal of that black soil and the pottery shards, but the rings were nowhere to be seen.

With an exasperated huff, I felt around inside the bag, sure they must have just missed the container, but they weren't there either.

Perplexed, I reached inside the artefact box, fingers gingerly exploring the narrow space, trying to avoid nicking myself on the corner where the metal coil was embedded. I felt the cool touch of the rings at the far end of the box, but they didn't budge. Were *they* what the metal was stuck on?

My index and middle finger slid through the hoop of the rings, and I felt them give. Emboldened, I tugged harder and the rings came free easily. I rocked back on the stool and nearly toppled over.

The bag dropped, followed by a metallic clang on the floor.

There, laying on the floor, was the straight full-length blade that had almost killed me in the street tonight. The metal gleamed.

"This cannot be." I reached for my bag, lifting and inspecting it. Sure enough, the metal coil was nowhere to be seen.

My gaze darted between the bare knife blade to my bag and back again.

"How …?" I breathed, unable to compute.

I looked at the two rings on my fingers, staring at the strange striations on the pale metal knuckles. They seemed no worse for wear, which didn't make sense if they had been stuck to the spool of metal, or blade or whatever it was.

Taking up the dish rag again, I carefully lifted the blade for inspection. I told myself that it had caught on the rings and somehow twisted around them. When I yanked the rings free, the blade had sprung back into shape.

Impossible.

It would require an insane tensile strength, not to mention heat, to bend a blade like that.

Further, the blade wasn't supporting my theory. The whole thing was completely intact and unblemished, right down to the tang. The holes punched into it, for the handle lugs were smooth and unbroken. There were no stress fractures or burring. It was in pristine condition.

I recalled the knife-wielder holding up his naked handle, and I found myself sharing in his shock.

My gaze drifted to the strange rings on my fingers, and a surge of curiosity swept over me. Professor Lowe's words bubbled to the surface.

Something else. Something very important.

I felt a sudden urge to reunite the rings and the blade. It was only the rational, scientific thing to do — test the phenomenon. Like a child holding a live wire, I wanted to see some sparks.

I placed the blade on the countertop, and then very gradually, I brought the rings to the blade.

Other than the clink of metal kissing metal, nothing.

Perhaps more force was needed. I pressed it down

harder. Still nothing happened. I tried raising my hand and moving it around before touching the two together. Maybe kinetic energy was the key. Nothing but a slightly louder clinking sound. Then I remembered the blade had been between the two rings so I tried placing it there again. Still nothing.

After more nothing and that irritating metal-on-metal noise, I yanked my hand away in disgust. In a fit of bad temper, I slapped my ringed hand down on the countertop.

The knife blade skidded away several inches as though frightened by the sound.

I stared in shock, then rushed to get a notepad and a pen out. It was time for some experiments.

I COULDN'T SEE.

Something hot and heavy pressed down on my face, keeping my eyes from opening. No matter how I pushed at the thick pliant mass, more of it slid down, keeping me blind. I jammed my fingers upwards, trying to stem the tide, and I felt it flowing like sand around my outstretched hands.

With a panicked scream, I realised it was surging down past my clawing hands to cover my nose and mouth. It swallowed my head, and with a painful, mocking slowness, it moved for the rest of me. I struggled as more and more of it rolled over me, heading towards my feet.

It was sinking over me, or I was sinking into it, plunging head first into the thick, cosy depths, and …

I realised, realising … this was comforting. I was safe. I was hidden.

But hidden from what?

Then the heat grew, no longer comforting but sweltering, then burning. I wasn't in a safe place. I was in an oven, a furnace.

I still couldn't see, and I felt my skin beginning to blister and bubble.

Suddenly, the dense material scattered in every direction, as though it couldn't stand to touch me a moment longer. With this sudden departure came the return of my sight and gravity. I lurched downwards, seeing a landscape of jagged mountains, darkly lustrous and unnaturally sharp. In the seams between these razored monoliths were vast, slow-running rivers of slag. Throbbing, angry red slop, winding and moving in a dozen contradicting directions.

And I was falling towards one of these slag-filled rivers.

The burning air whistled past my ears, becoming a terrible, condemning word.

TRAITOR!

I STARTED awake to the buzzing of my phone and promptly kicked the stool out from under myself. I slid unceremoniously off the countertop where I'd been lying, scattering my notebook and writing utensils.

Hitting the floor with a hard, dull thud, I sat there, staring and blinking up at my kitchen counter. My phone rumbled again, sliding across the countertop, working its way to the edge. Numbly, I registered it was falling as it plummeted into my bag, which lay in a formless lump on the floor. From within the folds of the crumpled bag, the alarm continued to buzz.

My body ached from having fallen asleep in a slumped position. I gave a symphony of groans as I crawled over to the bag. I was terrified to learn the time, scrunching my eyes shut as I turned the phone around. I opened one eyelid.

6:00am

I collapsed onto the floor again, the phone hoisted in victory. Six! I could get to work on time. There was a distant throb in the back of my head I was sure would blossom into a full-blown tension headache, but I was going to walk through those museum doors with my pounding head held high.

I didn't have any more time to celebrate, and I staggered to my feet. Rubbing my eyes and yawning, I spotted the notebook with pens and pencils scattered around it. My gaze wandered up from the notebook to the bare knife blade on the countertop, and I raised my hand to stare at the rings, still on my right hand.

So, last night had happened after all. It hadn't been part of the crazy dreams.

I didn't feel so steady on my feet as I scooped up the notebook. There, in black and white, in my own handwriting, detailed the dozens of experiments I'd done last night with the rings and the blade. I'd concluded whatever the rings were made of did not react to any direct physical stimulus.

With too little sleep and wired with the madness of the night, I considered the stimulus was psychological — reacting to my thoughts and feelings.

It had been small at first, just nudges and pulls, no doubt my own disbelief making things more difficult. But millimetres at a time, I began to move the knife blade across the counter. I measured fastidiously each time, recording my results in the notebook, but eventually I found I could, with a little mental effort, 'will' the blade across the length of the countertop with one push, and then back again with one pull.

I was so thrilled with this discovery the next push sent the knife flying towards my electric kettle, but with an outstretched hand and a flex of will, I stopped the blade mid-air. I'd relaxed my mind and body with a gasp and let the blade rest on the countertop. It now sat where I'd left it.

It would have been past one in the morning when that happened, and the fatigue of the prior day hit me like a cement truck. I'd lain there staring at the knife blade and the rings until my eyelids became too heavy to hold up.

Rather than grappling with the enormity of what I'd discovered, I got ready for work. Discovery or no, I needed to keep Shelton off my case.

I tucked the notebook into my bag, followed by the blade, then the container full of soil and pottery and finally the rings, placing them in a snug side pocket. I took three steps from the bag and stopped, looking back over my shoulder, feeling an overwhelming compulsion to go back and put the rings on.

"Next thing you know I'll be looking for Hobbits," I muttered as I stripped down and hopped into the shower.

The warm water was good for my throbbing head, and helped my nerves as well. As I scrubbed my scalp, I sorted through the realities of the day ahead.

I couldn't take the rings back, not now. This was more than just an archaeological discovery. It was a scientific revelation. Metal which provided a conduit for mental signals to alter magnetic fields! The fact it seemed to be thousands of years old only made it more amazing.

Thinking you've nothing to learn from the old ways reveals you've learned nothing at all, my mother used to say.

"Don't you know it, mum."

I still had so much to learn, test and explore. It was going to take time, and that meant I had to find a way to keep the Archive software from sending an overdue alert. I thought about checking the box in, minus the rings, but then strange Professor Lowe came to mind. I assumed he was a scoundrel or con artist but maybe not. What would happen when he came for the box, after having said something to me, and the rings were gone?

This musing caused me to wonder why he was keeping the rings to himself. This kind of discovery would make a scholar world famous. Why hide it in a pile of dirt and broken ceramics?

This was getting complicated.

I finished my shower and went through the motions of getting dressed as quickly as I could. It was already half-six. All this thinking was slowing me down.

I was going to have to put the Archive set on the back burner and hope that Shelton didn't notice. That might give me a few days, maybe as much as a week or two to do more tests. Maybe I'd even show the rings to Professor Schottelkirk. With her approval, we could put these mysterious little relics under some more granular tests and get an idea of what they were made of.

I rushed about making a cup of coffee, putting the kettle on and popping a filter into the pour-over. I ground my coffee beans earlier in the week, and so I had plenty but couldn't find the spoon I usually kept near the kettle.

I spied the vagabond utensil in a far corner, nestled between the extra plastic food containers I'd gotten out. It struck me as funny that I'd even been able to notice it, a dull glint in a mound of pastels.

Mindful of the time, I stretched a hand towards the spoon, one hand in the overhead cupboard, groping for a mug. I only saw a flash before something sailed up the length of my extended arm and struck me in the jaw. My teeth clicked together.

"Ow."

The hand in the cupboard knocked one mug over and sent another tumbling to the counter, where it shattered in a spray of chunks and slivers. A moment later, nursing my jaw, the spoon landed on the floor with a rattle.

The only sound in the flat was the rumble of the electric kettle.

Blinking stupidly at the spoon and massaging my injury, I looked at my hand, expecting to see that I'd forgotten I was still wearing the rings.

My fingers were bare.

Could there have been some residue, some trace elements from the rings? No, I'd just showered, unless the residue had been absorbed into my pores, but that would mean it was inside of me!

Fingers quavering, I stretched my hand over the spoon, and just as I had with the blade, focused my mind and willed it upwards.

The spoon flew into my outstretched palm.

I choked back a sob, fingers curling around the handle. As more of my skin came into contact with the metal, I became aware of a faint vibration. As I stood there staring at the utensil, my horror and awareness of the resonance grew. The metal in the spoon was 'singing to me.'

I yelped and threw it down.

It hit the ground and — in response to my rejection of what had just happened — flew across the room to strike the wall … hard enough to gouge the drywall. Dust sifted to the floor.

I stared at my hands and bit back another scream.

What is happening to me? What have I done?

Chapter Seven

I made it to work on time (without coffee), but was not in a productive mood.

Anytime I touched something made of metal — a handrail or a two pence coin in my pocket — I felt the resonance of it singing to me. And each and every time that happened, I wondered what sort of contamination had taken place. Was it radiation? Metal poisoning? Some cerebral chemical alteration?

I was no biology major, but I knew that something which caused such drastic changes would have side effects. It might be cancer, sepsis, organ failure or just plain insanity, but I was quite sure developing a mental connection to the base elements around me was not good for my health. Maybe that was why the ancients did not use such artefacts. Maybe they discovered the power of this strange metal, but soon learned it came at a terrible cost and so hid it away or cast if off.

"You don't know anything," I muttered as I swiped in. "Not yet."

Tariq looked up from the screen and smiled. "Morning, Ibby. Sorry, didn't catch that. Don't know what?"

My attention snapped to my immediate surroundings. I hadn't even realised I'd been speaking out loud. "I … ermm, that is …"

Tariq looked mildly concerned and completely unaware that the watch in his pocket — the one from his grandfather (a railway conductor) — was singing a song. It was our running joke to ask Tariq what time it was. He never failed to pull the watch out and remind me who it had once belonged to. It was sweet that he and his grandfather had been close, but given half a chance, I would smash that watch to pieces just to silence it.

But I knew it wasn't the watch. It was the sterling silver casing, the hardened bronze gears, the spring steel ribbon, the …

"Oi, Ibby!" Tariq waved a hand in front of my face. "You okay?"

I shook my head, trying to focus and ignore the song. I had been staring at (well, more 'through') his pocket. I must have looked like a complete loon.

"I'm sorry." I pasted my best tired smile on my face and tilted my head just to sell the look. I'd seen Jackie do it, and I was rewarded when Tariq's expression changed to a look of pity and relief.

"Burning the candle at both ends, are you?"

I nodded slowly and adjusted my bag as though it was incredibly heavy. "Life of the student intern."

Tariq shook his head with a smile and clicked his mouse to confirm my check in. That done, he gave me another pitying look. "Take care of yourself, Ibby."

I bobbed my head. "You too." Then shuffled towards the elevator.

Once inside, I stood in the very centre of the lift, trying

to block out the intense reverberating waves battering me inside the metallic box.

I MADE it to my workstation, miraculously, and took a moment to stand and breathe.

The tube and the elevator had been the worst, but every bit of metal I got close to twanged steadily like an out-of-tune instrument. I could feel a dull throb from the scissors and stapler in the cubbies, my archaic computer giving off an unpleasant hum. It was like having new, sensitive skin. Each time my new sense buzzed and prickled, I tried to adjust to it, but then another tingle rushed in from another direction. I was never comfortable, never at ease, and on top of that, I worried some metal missile would fly at me from nowhere … like the spoon. It was maddening.

There, in the little island of light at my desk, I breathed in and out. I mentally pushed back at the encroaching auras, trying to drive them away. The resonances didn't stop, but they shifted.

With a soft gritting shoosh, the computer slid an inch across the desk. In the cubbies below, the scissors and stapler clacked and scraped. My hackles rose and I backed off. If I pushed much harder, I was going to send things flying, and that was not going to decrease the stress in my life.

I decided that instead of pushing back, maybe I should let them in. Maybe I just needed to let myself desensitise naturally. A nagging voice in my head said it could also lead to insanity, but a louder voice suggested I was nearly there already.

I'd gone from family stress to work stress to accidental

crime to creeping fear to mugging interrupted. And now I was experiencing a phenomenon from exposure to a mysterious artefact that had done something to me.

Yeah, madness was on the bloody horizon.

My initial attempt to let myself adjust without fighting it was like plunging into a whirlwind. I had to grip the table to stay on my feet. I reeled, and fought nausea as my mind was pulled in all directions. With a strength I didn't know was there, I pulled myself back from the overloading storm of sensation.

Okay. Too much.

Next, I tried to focus on one individual resonance (the scissors), not fighting or resisting it but listening to its tune, letting it wash over me. It was strange, uncomfortable, but little by little, the discomfort gave way to a kind of familiarity. Like running your fingers over something commonplace in the dark. With the scissors settling into a comfortable 'shape,' I focused my attention on the stapler and did something similar. Then the computer, with its myriad of tones, which took longer.

I tried to quantify the nearby resonances, giving them definition. The dense alloys in the scissors were not like the thinner composites in the stapler, and both stood separate from the more complex interconnected metals that made up the ageing computer. They felt different because they 'were' different, but as I began to categorise those differences, I began to understand how there were similarities, categories.

Could I be sensing the very nature of the metal? What elements were present and in what ratios? How was I picking them up? Magnetic fields? Low-level radiation? Even if it was one of those, how could my mind make such a distinction?

And for the hundredth time: *What had those rings done to me?*

I placed my bag on the table and fetched out the rings. They somehow felt heavier in my hand, but that wasn't the strangest thing. In spite of being made entirely of metal, the rings gave off no resonance at all. They felt no different than plastic.

I slid the rings onto my fingers and then held them up. "You'd better not have given me a brain tumour."

Once the rings were on, the surrounding resonances were somehow clearer, not as invasive. Like distorted ambience noise, as they grew in clarity, they became less disruptive, and I could reach out further and understand them. A nagging tingle above me resolved into the network of copper wiring running from the light overhead like strands of an immense spider web. A bass rumble that shook beneath me originated from the monolithic steel beams that braced the floor and the walls. Sandwiched between layers of concrete, I could feel them, steady and stalwart. Their solidity was almost comforting.

So, things were easier with the rings, I mused. Sharper, more precise.

"You can admire jewellery on your own time, Ms Bashir," a painfully familiar voice announced from the gloom. "But while you are here, I insist that you *stay on task*."

Dr Shelton stepped into the light, his mouth set in a disapproving frown. His eyes gleamed wickedly behind his glasses. I'd been so intent on the rings I hadn't noticed his approach.

I scrambled for something to say and came up empty.

"Is your slack-jawed silence an indication that you don't actually *know* what your task is, Ms Bashir?"

I realised with horror I was holding the rings out in

front of myself, begging Shelton to notice them. I lowered them, fighting a near overpowering urge to hide them guiltily behind my back.

"Dr Shelton, I … that is … I didn't mean …"

Dr Shelton's features spread into a cold, humourless smile as I stuttered.

Heat blossomed in my cheeks.

"You didn't mean to get caught, is that it?" He raised a thin brow. "No, I don't imagine you did, but that is the odd thing about the lazy and irresponsible. They never believe their shirking will be noticed, even though it always is." He smiled, grimly. "Eventually."

Lazy? Irresponsible? The words burned, and it took a considerable amount of self-control to keep my tone even.

"I meant to say I didn't intend to break protocol. The packaging was damaged and so I …"

"Stop right there!" His eyes widened with incredulity. "I've heard enough."

My mouth clamped shut, the blood drained from my face. I realised only then Shelton had thought these were 'my' rings, but now …

"Are you telling me those gaudy things on your fingers are artefacts?"

I wanted to lie. But Shelton or not, I'd hedged on the truth enough with this business, and now was as good as any to come clean. It had been my plan to all along, so …

"Yes, sir." I took the rings off and set them on the desk.

Shelton glared as though willing me to melt into a pool of tears, but I only stared back, unwilling to give him the satisfaction. My career was over before it had begun. The discovery of a lifetime would be snatched up by someone else. I would probably never see my uncle again, but I was not going to let the likes of Adrian Shelton break me. Not today. Not ever.

"I had my doubts about you from the beginning Ms Bashir, but I never pegged you for a liar."

Liar?

I blinked at him. "I don't understand."

Shelton's voice was a patronising sneer. "Of course you don't. Come now, at least grant me the respect of dropping the act now that I've seen through your pathetic ruse."

He thought I was making this up?

"Sir, you don't understand —"

"No!" Dr Shelton's voice rose to a near shriek, so sudden and strident it shocked us both. For a moment, we only stared at one another. He with that acid glare, and me like a startled marsupial.

He cleared his throat. "It is *you* who do not understand. Unlike you," he said, hissing, "I take my job very seriously, and have done so for as long as you have been alive. That means I am familiar with all the exhibits and nearly all the artefacts." He glanced at the rings and back at my face. "That *thing* does not belong in any of the exhibits. I can easily deduce it is not remotely consistent in make and material to any other piece whose period they are mimicking, and mimicking badly, I must say."

I was unable to believe what I was hearing. He truly thought I was trying to pass off costume jewellery as an artefact. For what purpose? To get noticed? Promoted, perhaps?

But he wasn't done.

"I would bring this to your Proctor as well, but I'm certain you would only lie, because that is, apparently, what you do." He flapped a hand towards the rings in disgust. "But make no mistake, Ms Bashir. I am watching you. Dishonesty in this field ruins careers and spoils the trust of donors and the public. I will not tolerate it. Tread very carefully, miss, very, very carefully."

He stood trembling with anger, nostrils flaring with outrage and contempt, then smartly turned on his heel. My mouth felt glued shut as my mind spun.

"Get back to work," he growled over his shoulder, and stalked away.

IT WAS some time before I did get back to work.

I tried and failed to process the lashing Dr Shelton had delivered. He didn't believe the rings were part of the collection, and — if Lowe's ramblings were correct — then Shelton was actually right. This conveniently took nearly all the pressure off me. I didn't need to return something that didn't belong to the museum in the first place. I decided as soon as my shift was over, I would go to Professor Schottelkirk with the rings. She'd know what to do.

I would hold off on the metal manipulating business, at least at first. The rings and their craftsmanship should prove enough of a discovery to get me out from under Shelton's thumb. And the best part was, that after his little tantrum, Shelton would look a fool to question how I came across the rings. After all, I had tried to tell him about them, hadn't I?

There was still the matter of Professor Lowe though, and that matter came to the forefront when I booted up my computer.

As I waited for the antiquated machine to awaken, I slipped the rings back on and breathed a sigh of relief as the hum of the metals around me became manageable.

I was going through my usual routine of opening the database when the interdepartmental messaging system popped up with a notification. That in and of itself was odd, because the system was old, cumbersome and if museum staff needed to communicate, they usually sent emails.

There was a single unopened message from the porter's front desk. The time read 1:27am, which meant it had come from a night porter.

Bemused, I clicked on the message and read:

Ms Bashir,

I'm not familiar with the types of games you like to play with the porters on the day shift, but in the future, I would appreciate it if you toned it down. I've got nothing against a good joke, but that went too far.

I was very concerned for your safety so I searched the entire museum. I would've called the police if it weren't for Charlie, who explained sometimes the scholarly staff like to take the mickey. You had me going, but please let me in on the joke before you leave.

I heard you and Shelton had a go at it earlier, so I've made no formal report, and even Charlie doesn't know it was you who told me. What I'm saying is that no one knows, and I'd like to keep it that way, but if you try this with someone else, they might not be so understanding.

Be careful, Miss.

Cheers, Marcus

CONFLICTING feelings helixed around in my stomach at the messages, both overt and subtle. Marcus thought I'd played a trick on him. He hadn't mentioned it to Shelton, thanks heavens, and — most interestingly of all — he hadn't found Lowe.

The museum was large, but points of access were closely monitored, and Marcus was not new to the job. He should have found Lowe, or at least been informed if someone tried to get out without swiping. Could he be exaggerating about his efforts to make me feel bad? I didn't know Marcus that well, but he didn't strike me as the type. Yet, how could Lowe have slipped past him? Had he stayed here all night?

I felt a surge of paranoia and couldn't resist another visual sweep.

Who was this man? Some sort of master thief or spy, as though this were the movies? Had he gone back to Archives to search for what he misplaced? What would he do when he found it wasn't there?

Heart beating erratically, I made my way to the interoffice phone by the exit. The shadows between the shelves seemed to darken. I told myself to stop being silly as I punched in the extension for the porter's desk.

"Front desk," McPhee drawled.

"McPhee, it's Ibby."

McPhee made a grunt of recognition.

"Look, I know it is strange. But do you happen to have Marcus's cell number up there?"

There was a pause and a sigh. "Why?"

"Because …" I said, scrambling, my attention still torn between the phone and keeping an eye out for some lurking assailant. "Because, last night I was rude to him, and … and I wanted to apologise."

Another wheezy noise after a pause. "Why don't you tell him tonight?"

I ground my teeth together in frustration. "I can't."

"Why not?"

The building pressure slipped into my voice. "I just can't. Are you going to give me the number or not?"

A longer pause this time, then another windy sigh followed by a string of digits. I made him repeat them as I punched them into my phone.

"No good, though," McPhee grunted.

"What?" Then remembering my story, "Marcus is holding a grudge?"

"Nope. Sleeping."

I looked to the ceiling in exasperation. Of course. Marcus was a 'night' porter. Duh.

"I'll just leave a message. Thanks, McPhee."

The line clicked to the dial tone.

I hit call and stood with my back against the wall, drawing a sense of strength from the steel beams around me.

The phone rang several times then bludgeoned my ear with the screams of badly distorted electric guitars. I winced, pulling the phone away several inches.

"Hallo?"

"Marcus?" Still holding the phone away as shredding rock music blasted on.

"Who's this?"

"Ibby," I said as someone started bellowing along with the raging instruments.

"Who?"

"IBBY BASHIR," I shouted and then winced.

The change in Marcus's tone was instantaneous. "Oh, Ibby, I mean, Ms Bashir. Hey, how are you?"

The music escalated into a sonic jackhammer.

"Are you at a rock concert or something?"

"What? Oh, the music, hold on." He shouted a colourful phrase through the music, and a moment later it cut off. I heard several male voices raised in outrage before Marcus was back on the line.

"Stuff it, mate. I'm on the phone." He came back to the line. "Sorry, Miss Bashir."

"Call me Ibby." I brought the phone back to my ear. "I'm glad I didn't wake you."

"No, no worries. I hit the gym right after work."

I checked the clock on my phone. "Marcus, you've been at the gym for almost three hours?"

An embarrassed silence, all the more deafening for the lack of the brutalising music.

"Well, yeah … uh, you know … Is there something I could help you with, Ms Ibby."

I cleared my throat, suddenly self-conscious. "I got your note."

"Oh." A thick pause. "I'm sorry if it came off as rude. I'm not mad. I just … well, if you tried it with someone else, you'd be in trouble, is all."

A sharp pang of guilt. "Did you really end up searching the whole museum?"

"Yeah, but it wasn't nothing, I mean anything. Really, it wasn't."

I bit my lip and fought the urge to smash my phone on the floor. How was this possible? Where was Lowe?

I collected myself, realising the silence had stretched on again. The hair on my arms spindled to a stand, and I was gripped by a strong feeling that it would be best to just apologise and be on my merry way.

"Ibby?"

"I'm here," I answered, forcing myself to sound calm and collected. "I just wanted to call and say I'm sorry, and to thank you for taking such good care of me, I mean us, well you know, the museum."

"Thank you, I appreciate that. I figured it out after I checked the cameras."

My gaze was roving the lanes between the shelves, but the mention of cameras brought me back hard.

"You pulled up the cameras?"

Marcus gave an embarrassed chuckle. "Yeah. Would've saved me a load of time if I'd checked those first."

A sense of cold unease deepened in the pit of my stomach. "How do you mean?"

"Well, I rewound the feed to try and find the guy. Charlie'd told me by then it was a prank, but I didn't believe him until I watched you get off the elevator alone."

It felt like the floor had fallen out from underneath me, the walls spun in my periphery.

"Alone?" I echoed hoarsely.

Marcus chuckled again. "Yeah, you really had me chasin' shadows, but when you strolled out of that elevator solo, I knew I'd been had."

Alone.

My mind refused to wrap itself around that single word. I stared across Collections, feeling a fresh surge of fear.

"Ibby?"

I licked my lips with a dry tongue. "Thank you, Marcus. I appreciate it. See you later."

"Yeah, cheers. Actually —"

Numbly, I hung up the phone.

Chapter Eight

I couldn't process what Marcus had said, so I diverted myself with mechanical tasks. Read, type, scan, sort and repeat. By the time I came out of my blissfully absent haze to check the time, I'd finished all the pieces from the French Revolution exhibit. Looking at the stack of neatly arranged boxes on the trolley and checking the clock, I registered I had just enough time to take them back to storage before heading to university.

Why was I going to uni again? I didn't have lectures today. Oh, right … Professor Schottelkirk.

A current of excitement pulled my brain up to speed.

Alone. Marcus had seen me get off the elevator alone.

I shook off the haunting thought. Mad or not, I was taking these rings to my adviser, and together, we would reveal them to the world.

I practically sprinted my way to storage, threw the cart at the first bewildered staff member I saw and headed for the door, but I cursed and slid to a halt when I remembered I'd left my bag at my desk.

I still had the rings on. There was no point in hiding

them after Shelton's tirade so I almost decided to leave it. Then I remembered the naked blade tucked inside. Knife crime is serious business in London. If someone happened upon my bag and spotted the blade …

Muttering and cursing, I made my way back.

My bag was on the work table where I'd left it, but a piece of brown cardstock lay on top. Bold Piccadilly script screamed a headline, set over a picturesque sepia-tinted photo of an old tube station with people lining up at its entrance.

Picking it up, I held it before disbelieving eyes and read:

GRAND OPENING
BRITISH MUSEUM STATION
COURTESY OF THE BRITISH MUSEUM
AND THE UERL
Est. 1912 A.D.

I could barely keep my hands steady enough to unfold the thick stationery as it opened into a map of the London Underground framed by various images. At the centre of the map sat the British Museum Station, with connections branching out to the wider London Underground. I didn't recognise any of the connecting stations until I found Covent Garden.

Words delivered in a silvery, posh accent sprang to mind as I stared at the map.

If you find anything, please stop by the British Museum Station. Oh, but you will need a map, wait right here, I'll fetch you one.

Lowe had said that, right before vanishing into the administration wing.

Lowe — the man who did not exist.

If he didn't exist, then where did this map come from?

Was this proof that I wasn't mad or just my mind desperately clinging to its delusions? The texture of the heavy stock told me the map was real, but people who were insane saw and heard and even felt things that weren't there. Didn't they?

"Bloody hell!" I mashed the panels of cardstock together before chucking it into my rubbish bin. I didn't have time for this right now.

Shouldering my bag, I went to meet Professor Schottelkirk.

"SIMPLY EXTRAORDINARY!"

Professor Schottelkirk's reaction to my discovery was the best thing I'd heard in a long time. I beamed.

I'd met her at one of the cataloguing labs where students practised the techniques we would one day use in museums and university labs. Standing there with a respected archaeologist as she exclaimed over my discovery was quickly becoming the best moment in my entire life.

"I can't believe you just stumbled across this in … where did you say it was?"

It took me a second to stop basking and realise she'd asked me a question. "Oh, an archived container with some bits of early Hittite pottery. Shelton, erm, Dr Shelton thought I was playing some kind of trick."

My adviser held up one of the rings with a pair of rubber tipped tweezers.

"I'm no Near East expert, but I've only seen intricate metalwork like this in artefacts that had the benefit of modern metallurgy. The apparent composition suggests early Bronze Age." She took another few seconds to scrutinise them before setting them down on the table. She stepped back and pursed her lips. "Have you had a chance to put these under any tests?"

The change in the mood was palpable. Or was that just me? "No, I haven't. Use of the labs is only for those in the department. Dr Shelton would never give me access."

"No," she said, musing absently, her eyes looking far away. "He wouldn't."

I wanted to ask her what she was thinking, why she suddenly seemed so concerned, but I pulled back. If she wanted to say something, even something I didn't want to hear, she would say it in her own time.

Professor Schottelkirk paced around the table, her expression inscrutable.

"And with it being misplaced like that, I don't suppose you have any documentation or any clues to its provenance?"

I opened my mouth, desperate to give justification to the suggestion I smelled behind the question, but then decided against it. I shut my mouth and shook my head.

Schottelkirk mirrored my shaking head and then met my eyes. Her scrutinising scowl softened. "Ibby dear, please understand. I'm not doubting you, but we have to be cautious. Nothing appears out of thin air."

I felt a familiar weight settle over me. It took tremendous effort not to replay Meredith's words. I watched Professor Schottelkirk, bracing myself. "What should we do?"

She looked at the rings and then at me with that professorial potency which made her such a rock star in my eyes.

"We need to run some tests. We can hypothesise all we want about cuneiform styles and alloy striations, but until we have test results, no one will take us seriously."

That was remarkably better than I had any right to hope for. She hadn't dismissed them the way Shelton had, and — amazingly — was willing to invest resources. Sparks of hope burst anew in my chest.

"Along with the usual tests for early Bronze Age finds," Schottelkirk went on, "there is a new method pioneered by the University of Valencia: Voltammetric dating. It requires literal nanograms of material, so the rings will remain unscathed by it."

I vaguely recalled another professor mentioning the method in a distant lecture. It involved electric currents and trace amounts of corrosion, which I doubted the rings possessed, but we could cross that bridge when we came to it. For the moment, it was enough that she had a way to verify the discovery.

"While that is going on, we should compile a typological examination. The snobs at Cambridge will pick apart whatever we put together, but most respectable scholars won't look at anything without a legitimate typology attached."

Here she stopped, and her gaze returned to me.

"Ibby, I think it best if we keep this between us." Her smile was grave. "And I think it best we get something to write with. We have a lot of work to do."

I grinned. "Yes, ma'am."

EVERYTHING WAS SET IN MOTION.

Schottelkirk kept the experts we needed to work with in the dark. Thanks to them owing her a favour, they agreed to run the more technical tasks quietly. I was shocked at the ease with which she brokered these things. I never would have suspected she had skill in clandestine undertakings, but one by one, she removed obstacles, setting the wheels of modern archaeology spinning.

"Tact and timing are going to be everything," she explained as she walked me to the tube.

The rings were in my bag again, though not without a good deal of back and forth. Despite how they helped me sort the metallic songs (which I was getting used to now, as they were constant), I'd wanted to store the rings at the university. I'd suggested one of the sample lockers or a secure lab. Schottelkirk would have none of it. Either she would keep them or I would. The risk of accidental discovery was too great.

So, I told her I'd be happy to hang on to them. Maybe, there would be a chance for a decent night's rest, for once.

"As marvellous as this find is," she was saying, "we still have an uphill battle. We are going to need to insinuate ourselves with some people in the community. I'm afraid that will take some time, most of my liaisons are in further east antiquities, but I'll get it sorted. Contacts are never out of reach if you know where to look."

It was sounding more like intelligence work than archaeology, but it was exciting all the same. "I'm just eager to get my teeth into some real archaeology."

Schottelkirk nodded, smiling at me with a sidelong glance. "That and so much more, Ibby, but you must understand one thing."

She stopped and took both my hands the way my mother used to. The difference was that my mother's fingers were thick and rough from years of labour, while Professor Schottelkirk's were delicate and smooth; though, she gripped my hands with surprising strength.

"It may seem like paranoid prattle, but you can't tell anyone about this. None of your lecturers, none of your co-workers at the museum, and no friends."

I hid a wince, remembering Meredith, and I wondered if I should mention her but decided against it. Meredith had told me to bury it, and as far as we were concerned it was, so there was no need, right?

"The fact is, Ibby," she continued, "archaeology has as much politicking and grandstanding as any other practice where people spend money. Bright stars wink out if they threaten bigger constellations, if you catch my sorry metaphor."

I did. It was an idea I was becoming accustomed to. A girl from the East End shouldn't have been so naïve, but I'd hoped things would be different. We were supposed to be scholars and scientists. Seekers of truth.

"I understand, Professor," I said. "Don't worry. I won't let you down."

Schottelkirk held my hands a moment longer and then drew me in for a hug.

I was so surprised I just stood there, a rigid post in her arms. No one had hugged me since … since my mother … I swallowed at the lump forming in my throat and failed to budge it. My eyes began to burn.

She released me with a smile. "We're going to do great things together, Ibby. Just wait and see."

"Thank you, ma'am," I replied, a little robotically.

I had to get away from her before I fell apart. With a stiff smile and a wave, I ducked into the stream of people heading into the underground.

On the way home, hot, silent tears ran down my face.

Chapter Nine

I made it home, ate a few bites of *kisra*, a Sudanese fermented bread, and collapsed into bed. I was exhausted in a way I hadn't been since my parents died; a weariness so deep even my soul felt tired. I told myself I should be happy with everything we accomplished, but the songs of metal all around chimed in to remind me I shouldn't relax too much.

Like the sound of a relentlessly leaking tap, the old pipes in the walls worked on my nerves until I was vibrating, not just from them but from every single metal item around me. The hinges on the kitchen cupboards, the bits of metal in my phone, the kitchen utensils in the drawers, on and on. It buzzed, whined and hummed like an insane choir of insects.

With a growl of frustration, I rolled over and grabbed my laptop, hoping Uncle was up for a chat.

Firing up the computer, I gritted my teeth against the sensations of the metals in the laptop. There was a subtle change to the tone as electricity flowed through the machine, metal swelling and moving with the currents.

With some concentration, I could process the metals one from another, and that made my metallic awareness more manageable, though it took effort. It was akin to threading each metal's tone through a mental needle. Different tones meant different kinds of thread, but some were close enough to share the same needle. Those threads of connection were taut, vibrating like guitar strings. A dangerous question followed the metaphor my mind concocted: what if I pulled on those strings?

Was that what I'd been doing when I'd willed the knife blade across the countertop?

A small icon blinked at the corner of the laptop's screen. I had a message.

I clicked it, and it drew up the browser with a regimented list of my past messages, most from Uncle Iry, several from Jackie and a few from co-workers and research partners. At the top was a video message from Uncle Iry. Clicking on the thumbnail, the player opened and presented his familiar face in an unfamiliar setting.

The walls behind him were an expanse of white plaster, where a painting of two men in a reed boat hung. Part of a blackwood banister sat at the left-hand edge of the screen. Every now and again, a person passed behind my uncle. Many of them seemed to be dressed fairly well, especially for Sudan.

Where was he?

"I'z on," an unfamiliar voice pronounced from somewhere behind the camera. I didn't recognise the accent based on the short sentence, but it wasn't Sudanese.

"Thank you, *sah*," Uncle Iry said to the voice, before looking back at the camera. "Ibby, great news, but also a little hard. The project schedule has been updated. My team begins work now, which means this is the last message I will be able to send you for some time. I wouldn't have been able to send this if it weren't for my manager. He was kind enough to let me use his work computer."

Uncle Iry, ever the grateful soul, gave a nod to the person behind the camera.

"The first few weeks will be busy, so please don't worry if I don't reach out. I'm fine. I just have much work to do. When I get a chance, I will contact you, of course. Until then dear one, please don't worry and have some fun. You work so hard, but you are still young. I wish …"

Here Uncle Iry broke off, looking up at something beyond the webcam. His face knotted with confusion and then he nodded several times. "Sorry, sorry, sah. Ibby, I have to go. I love you, and I want you to know everything will be —"

The video ended, frozen on Uncle Iry's reassuring smile for a heartbeat before returning to the inbox.

I held back a sigh that I was afraid would turn into a sob as I shut the laptop. I put it back in my bag, and in a fit of temper, shoved the bag away from myself. I shook my head in disgust and rolled onto my back.

I'd gone looking for comfort, hoping Uncle Iry's unmatched good cheer would rub off, but after that message, I felt far from cheerful. My mind sorted through a long list of worries, some more paranoid than others, but all perfectly legitimate. Updated time schedules and him leaving early meant someone was in a rush. Rushing meant cutting corners and making mistakes, the sort of mistakes that could get men hurt or killed.

And, what kind of person would let Iry send a video message to his only family, just to cut him off before he had a chance to finish?

I stared at the ceiling and ground my teeth. My thoughts scattered as dissonant metallic tunes filtered in.

My hands clenched into fists, then tightened, my knuckles popping. Finally, I sprang off the bed.

"Sod it!"

My room was only lit by the city lights outside the window. Going to my bag in the gloom, I fished out the rings. They glinted in the twilight of the streetlamps, beautiful and dangerous in a way I hadn't appreciated until then. As though they were beckoning to me to put them on.

I ran my thumb over the broken side before sliding them onto my fingers. The metallic songs fell into place with ease, becoming an almost soothing white-noise. Any one of them could be isolated, defined. I was beginning to think — as with Tariq's watch — if I concentrated, I could understand the metal I was sensing.

With the metallic droning dampened, maybe I could sleep. As I lay down on the bed, my body seemed to sink deeply into my lumpy mattress and relax.

I WAS FALLING AGAIN, through ashes and soot. Sparks and cinders flashed angrily around me.

At times, the cinders looked like angry eyes, glaring with the intensity of a blast furnace. Watching the glowing eyes distracted me from my plummet, but soon the rush of wind was too great. An enormous rumble erupted, like a splitting mountain. Looking down, I saw the hellish landscape. Desolate valleys shot through with churning, molten ore.

I screamed. Ash and soot coalesced into tendrils around me, and I watched, horrified as those black tendrils plunged into my open mouth. Choking and gagging, I coughed to expel the burned, gritty sediment, but it plunged into my body … forcing me to swallow it.

SILENCE, TRAITOR!

A voice burned in my mind and roared in my ear, filling the air around me.

FAITHLESS! MURDERER!

I was plummeting for the slag-flows but welcomed the annihilation, to escape the smothering soot.

NO ESCAPE! NO RELIEF! NO FORGIVENESS!

The dark crust on the runny metal below swelled, a molten glow visible through jagged cracks. Through teary eyes, I saw an immense pustule form on the surface of the flow I would land in. The growth ruptured in huge gouts of sizzling liquid.

Rising out of the wound came something too bright to see, giving a vague impression of incredible size and glittering metallic limbs. A mouth yawned beneath me, gaping with a blackness that shimmered with an endless, bitter heat. As I fell, I heard the sound of great engines working in that burning darkness, their gears gnashing and grinding.

I threw my arms out and kicked my legs, hoping for some way to stop the descent. The soot chased me down as I fell at last into a bottomless pit from which there was no escape.

MY BODY WAS COVERED with a frigid sweat as I jerked away, only to realise I could barely move.

Something … no, many somethings, pressed in on me, trapping me beneath my blanket so tightly I could only squirm. Fighting to stave off panic, I kicked my legs until I made it to a sitting position. Little clinks and ticks of metal on metal sounded in my ears.

I half-laughed and half-sobbed as I stared down at myself.

It was like someone had ransacked my apartment, and then — thinking better of it — returned all the items by dumping them on top of me as I slept. My bag, my electric kettle, a lamp, entire drawers holding my kitchenware, a pot and more all lay piled on top of me.

I propped myself up on my elbows, staring in disbelief. A buzzing sound issued from somewhere in the pile. I dismissed it as tones of metal, but then realised the buzzing was an actual sound, not a sensation, and that is when I also realised what was all over me.

Metal.

Every metal object that wasn't securely fastened down was on me. I gave another half-mad laugh, grateful that my landlord had bolted the minifridge to the floor. The morbid humour evaporated as the buzzing came again. I clued in that it was my phone.

I had one hand free and tried to shuffle my way to freedom, but something had shifted as I'd moved earlier, and now I was practically trapped. I glared at the assembled pile. Did I really own so many metal items that they pinned me in place?

"Oh, bollocks," I snarled and began using my free hand to clear the items away. But that was no easy thing either. The first thing I grabbed was a small pot in which I sometimes cooked *asseeda* — a kind of porridge — when I was really missing my mum. I knew how much it weighed, which was not very much at all, but when I went to push it away, it was like pushing on a huge stone block.

My father, as a mechanic, had loved tools, and though he did not have the same standard of workshop in the UK that he enjoyed while working in Sudan, he collected some tools. One was a telescoping magnet. It was powerful for something so small, and as a little girl, I'd once stuck it on the steel door that led outside our living complex. It had held fast, and even when I'd gotten Jarvy, the biggest, strongest boy in the building to help me, all we managed to do was bend the telescopic arm and scrape it a handful of inches. I had been terrified to tell my father. Money was scarce, and tools were not cheap. He'd marched me over to the door, and with a shake of his head, reached down and pulled the magnet off the door. I remember watching the muscles flexing under the taut skin of his forearm as he did so, showing the obvious, adult-sized strength it took to remove even such a small magnet.

The same feeling I'd had hauling that magnet was what I felt when I pushed on my *asseed* pot. Had I really magnetised all the metal things in my flat? To myself?

Wiggling the fingers of the hand still trapped under the blanket, I felt the rings. Maybe it wasn't such a wild theory after all. If I could draw things closer with the rings, why couldn't I push them away?

My phone buzzed again, and I was brought from the theoretical realm to the real world, one where I needed to get ready for work.

I remembered metal songs as strings fed through needles. I'd wanted to know what happened when I tugged. Hadn't I? No time like the present.

When I plucked them, the strings seemed willing to comply. The trash heap gave a sympathetic tremble.

My phone buzzed again, somehow angrier and more urgent than before, and my irritation flared. Mysteries like nothing any human had ever recorded were happening in my flat, and my damned alarm was intruding.

With a flash of petty indignation, I mentally grabbed the strings and threw the heap of metal away.

The result was instantaneous and catastrophic.

Like an erupting volcano, metal items flew everywhere, some at incredible speeds. My reading lamp spun end over end to hit the far wall. The bulb shattered spectacularly. My bag did several awkward rolls across the floor, like a lumpy tumbleweed. The kitchen utensils went everywhere, including a fork that whizzed past my eye and buried itself in the love seat. One of the pots shot straight at the window, and hit the centre frame. With a CRACK and a hollow BONG, it left an immense spider-web fracture in one of the panes.

Defiantly, my phone — still swaddled in the pocket of my trousers from the day before — spun in the air before plopping down next to me.

I fumbled to get my phone out, turned off the alarm and glared at the screen.

It was three minutes after seven.

With a series of unladylike expletives, I sprang out of bed, finally free. I yanked on yesterday's trousers and tried like mad to collect my thoughts. Could I still make it? If I ran like a madwoman, was there still a chance I'd get to work on time?

My apartment looked as though a bomb had gone off in it, so getting ready took longer than usual. By the time I was out the door, I couldn't bring myself to look at the time. I hoped Shelton was sick or had been hit by a double-decker, then kicked myself for such horrible thoughts.

Let the chips fall where they may.

"WELL, well, well. Ms Bashir, do you know the time?" Shelton sneered with pleasure in his beady eyes. He folded long, spidery fingers in front of his stomach. "My guess is not."

The chips fell squarely not in my favour.

I stood at the front desk in utter disarray, with not only the porters but staff members from Cataloguing, Collections and Filing looking on with abject pity. My humiliation had quite an audience this time.

The new exhibit lists were up on the bulletin board outside the doors to Administration, and everyone was checking what their workload would look like over the next few weeks. Meredith was there with the two knobheads, tea in hand, watching the train wreck unfold. Her eyes were soft but resigned.

"I said ..." Shelton began, but a sharp look from me drew him up short.

"I know the time as well as you do, sir. We both know I'm ten minutes late." I couldn't prevent the sass. It came out like a surprise belch.

Shelton's nostrils flared, and I found his irritation oddly satisfying. I stood a little taller and met his eyes proudly, almost dismissively.

"If you'd like to impose consequences, please go ahead, but I'd like to get to work. I have much to do before the lectures this afternoon."

I swiped my card before he could say anything and moved towards the elevator.

Shelton moved with feline quickness to stop me. Rigid and looming, he peered down his nose. "Who do you think you are?"

"Steady on, sir," a voice called from the assembled co-workers. Dr Shelton dismissed the voice with a sharp wave of his hand.

I stared up at him in stony silence, jealous of his height advantage, but I was determined to not let him sense any intimidation. He could smell fear, like bees and dogs.

His eyes narrowed hatefully, his lip curling into a snarl. "Do you think you are so special, so gifted that the rules do not apply to you?"

Stung, I shook my head, holding his gaze.

"No? Then perhaps you think your age or inexperience should excuse you from the common decency of showing up for work on time?"

Again, I shook my head without letting my stare waver. I seemed to have lost my voice.

"Really," he said softly, cocking his head, snakelike. "Then what makes Ibukun Bashir so free, so untouchable? Your looks, your test scores, your gender, the colour of your skin?" He raised his voice. "Tell me, Ms Bashir. Explain it to us!"

He gestured to the crowd of staff frozen in place. My cheeks burned with embarrassment. Determined not to cry and just as determined to stand up for myself, I opened my mouth.

But Meredith stepped out from the crowd, one palm out. "All right. This is a conversation to be had behind closed doors."

Shelton bristled and turned cold eyes on Meredith. "I will handle this without any assistance from you, Ms Janssen."

Shelton turned his gaze and his whole body squarely to face me. Behind him, Meredith gave a little shiver of anger. With a slow exhale, she leaned forwards, her voice quiet. "Adrian, please, this does not look good."

Dr Shelton ignored her.

"Ms Bashir, you've yet to answer my question." Dr Shelton sniffed. "Please explain to all present why you feel free to insult both this institution and the many people who work here with your perpetual laziness and deceit."

The heat growing in my belly finally sprang to my tongue. "Lazy and deceitful?" I cried, outraged. "You pile meaningless work on me out of petty spite. Do you, *Doctor* Shelton, have nothing better to do with your time than henpeck, belittle and tyrannise interns?"

I was trembling and out of breath, but also exhilarated. Shelton stood rigid, his face reddening and eyes widening. He seemed unable to speak and that emboldened me.

"Clearly not," I went on, taking a step towards him, bringing us nearly nose to nose, "because that is all you seem to do. That is when you aren't lurking around corners like a miserly spectre, waiting to nag, jeer and bitch! You are nothing but a small-minded, ignorant brute! A pretender and a persecutor. But, I forgot," I sneered with dramatic irony, "that's your field of study. Isn't it? Excuse *me*, oh, great professor of vindictive bullying!"

Shelton rocked back on his heels, expression growing thunderous.

"That's enough," Meredith's voice pitched sharply at me this time, but it was barely audible as my heart hammered in my ears. "You had your say, so let's —"

"You, sir," I said, hissing the words, ignoring her and narrowing my eyes at Shelton. "You are everything which is provincial, rigid and backwards in this building, this country and this world. You are just the nearest of a long line of strutting and sneering tyrants in tiny sandcastles. If you weren't such a nuisance, you'd be laughable! A bloody joke. That's what you are."

Adrian Shelton's face was nearly purple with fury. I wondered if it was possible for a person to explode. I was nearly to the point of laughing at his trembling, swollen face, when a change came over him that made my blood run cold.

The furious pallor slid away, his eyes became glittering slits. A thoroughly wicked smile spread across his face. A viper's fanged grin would have been less venomous.

The rush of victory drained out of me as I realised what a mistake I'd made. With a sinking sensation, I followed his stare to my hand.

The rings glittered on my fingers.

In my rush to get to work this morning, I hadn't stowed them in my bag. My stomach clenched hard enough to make my legs quiver.

"Not even your bulldog, Schottelkirk, can save you this time," he said softly. "Falsifying a discovery is an act of criminal proportions."

I tried to recover that defiant fire, but it had guttered out completely, leaving me hollow except for an impending sense of dread. I covered the rings with my other hand.

Behind Shelton, I noticed Meredith's expression harden. She had seen the rings.

The little crowd of staff watched dumbly, knowing that something had changed in the scene they were witnessing. Everyone looked at me with a mixture of shock and perhaps fear. I was not one of them, not anymore. Shelton's public accusation had changed everything even if it wasn't true. I had somehow, irrevocably, become Other.

"I … It's …" The words squeezed out of my tightening throat as my vision began to blur. I looked at Meredith, a woman I respected and who'd always had a smile for me. I saw the face of a stranger. The hard lines of her expression seemed set at every angle against me.

"Meredith, please," I managed, "it's not true."

But she shook her head. "Ibby," Meredith said, her voice flat and cold. "You should leave."

"But … I …"

"Now."

It was all I could do to leave the museum without running and bursting into tears.

Chapter Ten

I walked the street, aimless and bereft.

How could I have forgotten about the rings? How could I have been so stupid?

I felt their weight on my fingers. I wanted to yank them off and hurl them away. I could have hurled them into the street to be smashed by a bus or chucked them down an open grate, condemned to the subterranean dark. I convinced myself I could do it if I really wanted. I could exercise a hollow but no less satisfying justice on the item that had brought such chaos, fear and pain to my life.

I could have, but something deep inside told me not to.

As I wandered down streets that were becoming more and more unfamiliar, I rationalised. Turning down an alley that smelled strongly of curry and wet sneakers, I began to enumerate the reasons aloud to the rings.

"Schottelkirk is connected. Just because a bridge is burned doesn't mean we can't get you out to the public. Even if my name can't be on the project at first, they won't be able to deny what the tests show. Once they realise … everyone will know Shelton accused me falsely."

On the street adjoining the alley, a metro police car shot by, sirens blaring. I jumped, wondering if Shelton had contacted the police. As the sirens faded into the general clamour of London, I shook my head at my own foolishness. The museum knew where I lived, where I went to school; if they wanted me arrested, they would send officers there.

My heart took its time returning to its normal rhythm. It was a few minutes and a turn down another alley before I resumed talking with the artefacts on my fingers.

"Besides, I'm an archaeologist, Shelton and Meredith be damned. I'm not going to throw an ancient treasure away just because I'm having a bad day."

Up ahead, where the alley opened onto the street, a few people stood sharing a smoke. They were speaking too low to understand, but their voices susurrated between the brick walls of the alley into a kind of hissing murmur. Half-consciously, I tightened my grip on my bag.

"Also, I'm going to need you to keep me sane. I can't imagine spending the rest of my life without metal, so you're my long-term sleep aid at the very least."

Approaching the alley mouth, the smokers were so engrossed with their conversation, they didn't make room for me to pass. I quickened my pace, intending to slip around them without having to walk between the streams of tobacco fog.

"Excuse me," I said to alert one that I was moving between him and the wall.

Both smokers — thickly built men in coveralls and dark windbreakers — turned towards me, effectively blocking off the alley with their bulk.

"Sorry," one said with a slight shrug of his meaty shoulders.

"I just need to get by you, gents," I answered, assuming he hadn't heard me.

"No, he means, sorry about this," the other explained as he dropped and stamped out his cigarette.

"What?" I turned to face him.

A hand gripped the back of my neck.

"This," hissed the voice behind me as the alley wall rushed towards my face. I managed to get my arms up in time to keep from smashing into the brick, but I still struck the wall hard enough to fill my eyes with stars and my head with cotton.

Someone stripped the bag from my shoulder and threw me to the ground, something my addled brain and unsteady legs were more than happy to comply with. Time took on a strange, syrupy consistency as I lay on the damp concrete, trying to makes sense of the dingy bits of rubbish in front of my vacant eyes.

A call from further up the alley, "Hey, you find it?"

The thick voice above me snarled a curse in frustration. "If I did, you think I'd still be shovin' my nose in 'er bag?"

Snorting chuckles came from two of them standing at the alley mouth.

"Stop sniffin' around fer panties, yeh perv. Get to the shiny bits," one chided, setting his partner to braying. "You can get your fill o' that later."

I heard the contents of my bag being dumped to the alley floor, the thunk of books, clatter of pens and the brittle clank of my laptop. The latter sound woke me from my stupor. With a throbbing pain in my arms and one shoulder, I dragged myself into a sitting position. I stared at the heap of my things, dazed.

"What are you doing?" My cheeks felt stuffed with cotton.

A tall man with a bull neck and chin like an anvil was

squatting over my stuff, hastily shaking whatever he held before roughly tossing it aside. "Nothin'," he growled, but it was to his partners, not an answer to my question.

One hooked his chin towards me, while the other fished out a fresh fag and hung it from his lips. "Check her."

My mind still hazy, I had just enough time to shift my gaze to the big mugger before he hauled me to my feet with one shovel-wide mitt.

"Up you go," he rumbled, one hand wrapped in the lapels of my jacket, while the other flicked out a switch-blade that looked almost dainty in his thick paw. He waved the blade in front of my eyes, letting me see the razor edge.

"You open that pretty mouth to scream, and I'll cut you a fresh windpipe, understand?"

Addled as I was, the most terrifying thing was not the threat itself, but the calm, almost workaday way he said it. He might have been talking about the weather or the latest football scores. Somehow, this cut through the rest of the fog, and the knife snapped into focus.

"You get it." He nodded from the other side of the switchblade. "Good girl, now let me see your hands."

Fear automated my responses. I straightened my arms, fingers extended. He took the hand that bore the rings, crooking the arm with the knife around it so he pinched my wrist inside his armpit. The blade still hung just in front of my face, as he grasped the rings, intent on removing them from my hand.

That same deep feeling, rooted in my very soul, quickened, and I began to struggle.

"No! Stop!" I screamed. The point of the knife came less than an inch from my eye.

"What did I say, lass?" His voice was as hard and pitiless as the razor-sharp steel.

Steel. A hard, vibrating song. A metal whose chord I'd threaded before.

The big man was talking again in that same deadpan tone that had chilled me to awareness. "Be smart, and no more of that ..."

He didn't finish his sentence. His eyes were drawn to the sinuous movements of his knife's blade. It stretched and curled like a shiny, probing invertebrate, its sharp head searching for a soft home.

"What the —" and then he screamed as a home was found, deep in his meaty hand.

He released me as my mind let go of the blade. The metal sprang back into its rigid, straight shape, and he gave another hiss of pain. He released my arm and lurched a step away from me, looking at the blade without its handle, now jutting from his hand.

I stood there gobsmacked by what I'd just done. Then the other two lunged towards me as their partner pitched against the wall, cradling his hand.

Spotting the switchblade handle on the alley floor, I mentally grabbed the pewter pins holding the wooden grip together and shoved, hard.

The handle rocketed forwards, and though I'd been aiming for the closest man's stomach, the handle struck him squarely in the groin. He gave a windy squawk and fell to his knees, clutching himself feebly.

The other man barrelled past, knocking his partner to one side as he reached out with both hands. His fingers brushed my sleeve as I threw my mind against the zipper of his slicker. There was a sudden hot, zipping sound as I yanked it upwards, and he gave a wet, strangled cry. He staggered backwards, pawing at his throat.

I looked at the three hulking men crumpled before me, and I felt something heady and surreal. These men, these brutes, now humbled, had been brought low by my will alone. The sensation, the realisation of it was immediate and powerful. It was like vindication, a kind of manifested conviction. It felt good, but more than good, it felt … right. I looked down at the rings and thought it seemed as if they were saying, *finally, she's figured it out.*

There was a snarled curse, and I turned in time to see the big, thick-voiced man yank the blade from his hand. With blood dripping, he spun and hurled the red length of steel. I sent it flying sideways with one flick of my hand. It buried itself in the alley wall.

He wasn't so easily dissuaded. Snarling another curse, he charged, one hand raised to smash me flat. He wasn't wearing a windbreaker, but the buttons of his open jacket provided excellent leverage to tug him off balance. His swing went so wide he stumbled past me and then, with a little more help from his buttons, smashed face first into the side of the building. He hit hard enough to make me wince. When he slid to the ground, I wasn't surprised he made no motion to get up.

I turned towards the other two, expecting to have to defend myself immediately, but they just stood there staring. The one nursing his groin looked from the handle in front of him to me and back again. The other, his zipper now limp with my attention elsewhere, rubbed at the purpling welts around his throat. Both stared at me in open terror.

Reaching out with my new sense, I laid hold of half a dozen pieces of metal detritus in the alleyway and willed them to rise up. They climbed into the air, hovering between me and what was left of my attackers, a brutal promise made without words.

"You boys should start running." A smile I couldn't help tugged at the corners of my mouth.

A second more of consideration, and both men bolted from the alley without looking back.

I let the hovering garbage hang for another moment before I relaxed, and the items pattered to the ground. A tremor travelled up my legs, then it wracked my whole body.

Shock. I must be in shock.

I was standing in a dirty alley with my bag emptied at my feet and an unconscious mugger behind me. If anyone happened by, I would have a hell of a time explaining myself.

Stooping on unsteady legs, I shoved my books and laptop into my bag without stopping to inspect them for damage. My whole body still quivering, I left the alley, doing my best to walk without falling.

I PLAYED the scene over and over in my mind as I walked the open thoroughfares.

What had I done?

With a power I barely understood, I'd disarmed and beaten three men. They weren't like the scrappy ruffians from the other night. All three, judging by their weathered features were in their thirties, if not older. The way they'd trapped me meant they were experienced, had foresight. The thought of veteran criminals executing violent and coordinated robberies was enough to make me feel ill, powers or not.

If they were random muggers, they wouldn't have passed up my laptop. Or my textbooks, which could be sold on-line for nearly a hundred quid apiece.

When the big one had declared "Nothin'" over my

emptied bag, I'd thought he meant nothing worth taking. But when he was told to check me …

"Let me see your hands."

A chill lifted the hair on the back of my neck. They'd been looking for the rings.

That was it. And if it weren't for the powers I'd inherited, they would have the rings right now. And what would have happened to me after they'd taken them?

The thought hammered me, and I staggered unsteadily to a conveniently placed lamppost.

People walked past, cars zoomed by, everyone going about their business. I clung to the post, the steel offering its comforting strength from beneath a thin layer of paint. My chest tightened. It was crippling to think that criminals — people I'd never met before, who didn't know me besides my name or what I looked like — were coming to take something from me, and they didn't care if I was hurt or even killed in the process.

I'd always known there were bad people, even evil ones. They needed to be avoided, like traffic or a crack in the pavement. They were there, and they could ruin your day or even be dangerous, but they'd never been *looking for me.*

Things had changed.

Someone had come for the rings.

But who? And how could they know I had them? Who might have told them?

The list was small: Shelton, Schottelkirk and Meredith.

It seemed impossibly out of character for the latter two to be involved in sending professional thugs after me, and Shelton as much as he was cruel and wicked, was really only a grandstanding bureaucrat. He wanted people to kowtow to his position, and he loved to lord his authority over his inferiors. I didn't believe he had the spine for something like this. Plus, he thought the rings were fake.

So why was this happening?

I straightened, one hand still on the streetlamp. The back of my neck prickled with a sense of vulnerability. I had to keep moving. I wasn't sure where I was going at first, but as I followed my feet, I realised I was headed to the university. I wasn't ready to descend into the tubes, the open sunshine feeling safer than the enclosed underground. Muscle memory to the rescue.

I'd been walking with a purpose, my head swivelling to survey my surroundings for the better part of fifteen minutes when my phone vibrated.

Message: Prof. Schottelkirk

Ibby, you need to come in. Now.

The fact I was getting a text message from my adviser was reason enough to be concerned as she despised cellular phones in general. This must be urgent, and though I knew it had to do with the encounter earlier, I was surprised she'd heard already. It wasn't even lunch time, and the academic machine was gearing up to grind and chew me properly.

I replied: **On my way.**

I was rewarded with another text.

Call me when you're close. Don't come to my office.

My pace quickened.

Chapter Eleven

I followed Schottelkirk's instructions to meet her at the records building, an austere collection of bricks that was older than many countries. I went in the side entrance where a foyer opened into a long hall. Photographs and paintings ran the length, each with a bronze plaque set beneath. Between each were glass-topped display cases inside which relics of the university's younger days sat mouldering. Lights hung from the vaulted ceiling, but only every other light was on. Swaddled in an artificial twilight left me feeling uneasy.

I sent a message to let Schottelkirk know I was waiting, omitting the fact I was anxious.

Unable to stand lurking in the shadows, I busied myself with the art hanging on the walls. Most of it depicted university faculty who — by dint of impressive title or actual effort — had brought esteem to the institution. A painting of one weak-chinned Professor Emeritus with a family name that sounded vaguely royal neighboured a black and white photo of a bushy-browed man, which in turn hung next to an assembled skeleton of … something. Nepotism and achievement strolled hand in hand down the hall. Once I'd accepted this was the case, it was almost fun to guess who were the real scholars and who were vapid figureheads.

I began to forget about my devastated career and the threat of violent criminals as I wondered whether Sir Ashley Igglesworth had contributed anything as head of the Sociology department, besides his fantastic surname and a head of hair that put both Einstein and Marx to shame. I stifled a giggle at a pudgy scholar named Weston, doing his best to look sagely as he stood next to a sarcophagus easily twice his height.

As I read the name of the tall man who stood on the right-hand side of the sarcophagus, opposite Weston, my mirth evaporated.

JAMES LOWE, NEAR EASTERN STUDIES (Right)

I read the name twice, before looking back to the photo to scrutinise the face there. The poor lighting concealed the familiar features, but the longer I looked the more I saw the peculiar man I'd encountered.

This was the man who had dodged Marcus's search as well as the security cameras. The man who had been with me as I'd stepped off the elevator *alone.*

The lack of colour in the photo made it hard to tell, but his hair had more than the shock of pure silver I'd seen, and perhaps the lines were not so deep. The differences were there, but they were matters of age, not identity.

I looked back at the plaque under the photograph, and my heart rocketed into my throat.

PROFESSORS HAROLD WESTON, EGYPTOLOGIST (Left)

and

JAMES LOWE, NEAR EASTERN STUDIES (Right)

1918

This photograph was nearly a hundred years old, and Lowe could not be a day younger than forty. There was no way he could be the same man!

Lowe must have had a son he shared a name with, but that didn't explain why he hadn't shown up on the CCTV. The longer I stared, the more impossible the son theory seemed. The uncanny similarity was beyond genetics. The lines in the face, the styling of his hair and even the uncomfortable way he stood rigidly for the photograph was an exact replication.

It had to be him, but what did that mean?

I was grappling with the implications when the door at the end of the hall opened. Professor Schottelkirk came flying towards me, hard heels snapping on the polished floor.

"Professor, what's going …" I stopped when I saw her.

Across one side of her face was a large bruise in shades of deep blue, purple and red. Her eyes were bloodshot and puffy.

"Oh, Ibby!" Schottelkirk sobbed, in a voice so small and scared that it shook me. I'd never heard her sound like that. She was a force, a champion of archaeology, a larger-than-life mentor. Now she seemed a thin, middle-aged woman at the edge of falling apart.

"What happened?"

"Oh, Ibby!" she repeated and pressed a hand to her mouth while hugging herself with her other arm. She was shaking like a leaf in a windstorm, her ragged breath whistling between curled fingers. The longer she looked at me, the more scared I became.

Shoving aside self-conscious thoughts about propriety, I wrapped my arms around her. She didn't resist, but pressed her face into my shoulder and let loose a flow of tears.

As I stood there holding her, making soft reassuring sounds, I mused over the abrupt role reversal. By rights, I — who'd been violently attacked twice within a few days, had been suffering under a vindictive weasel of a man and was an orphan in a vast city — should be the one being comforted. But the recognition came without bitterness or remorse. I was here, she needed comfort and that was something I could give. My own anxiety lessened in the face of her distress, as now I had a reason to be strong, to pull myself together.

Make it better by being better.

Schottelkirk's sobs subsided into soft sniffs, and she'd stopped shaking by the time I released her. She looked an utter mess, but the fragility in her gaze had lessened.

"Professor Schottelkirk," I said gently but with urgency, "tell me what's going on."

She looked about to fall apart again, but my gaze remained locked with hers, and she rallied.

"They took everything, Ibby," she blurted, and drew another shaky breath. "I didn't know … I mean, I didn't think. I'm so sorry. I interrupted them this morning as they ransacked my office. I didn't even have time to scream before one of them brained me."

She touched her head, and I noticed the bandage on her scalp. Her fingers trailed down to her swollen, discoloured face. "I must have struck my head when I fell. There was more than one of them. They knew what they were looking for, because they found everything."

Everything? What everything? My mind flailed to understand, but suddenly it came to me. I straightened, growing cold as I registered what she was saying.

Our work.

"I've also since learned they took everything from the labs and wiped all the records."

All the tests, all the typological notes, every bit of work we'd done on the rings was gone.

"They're going to come for the rings themselves. I'm sure of it. Do you understand, Ibby? It's only a matter of time before —"

"They've already tried," I said flatly.

Schottelkirk paled and gripped my forearm tightly, her fingers trembling.

"I got away, obviously. I don't think they have any idea where I am right now."

My adviser nodded mutely, but her eyes roved about like that of a spooked mule.

I had an idea what the answer might be, because of her apology, but I had to ask. "How did they know about them, Professor?"

Her lower lip quivered, and she shook her head, the gesture pitiful and childish.

I nearly lost my footing as she threw herself on me again, grinding her eyes into my shoulder as she sobbed. "It was me! Ibby, I'm so sorry, but it was me!"

She'd told someone, likely multiple someones, even after her insistence that I keep mum. I fought the urge to shake her. "We weren't supposed to tell anyone. Not friends, not colleagues, no one."

The edge in my tone caught Schottelkirk, and she drew back. I let go of her, watching with what I was sure were less than friendly eyes.

"It was for *you* to keep quiet," she sniffed, taking on a more strident tone. "You don't have the contacts, the clout, the skillset that I do. I've hobnobbed with politicians, deans and bloody royalty. This shouldn't have been any different!"

I reminded myself she was rattled and nothing good would come from scolding her, even if she was acting childish. "Who did you tell?"

She stiffened and brought a hand to her mouth again. "People I thought I could trust. Scholars and contemporaries who specialise in Near Eastern and Bronze Age studies. People we needed and whose expertise and reputation would keep us from being laughed out of every respectable institution! People we would have had to contact eventually anyway."

Something in her tone nagged at me. "Are they the only people you told?"

Her defensive façade began to crack. "There are a few, not even a handful of others, I may have hinted to." Her eyes tracked all over my face anxiously. "They are peers … I suppose, rivals of a sort. I thought a few words and a picture or two might remind them I was still a force to be reckoned with."

I took a step back, my hands coming up to cradle my head. I suddenly felt very tired, and my head was pounding. I moaned in disgusted disbelief and massaged my temples. I couldn't see Schottelkirk, but her shrill voice stabbed my ears.

"You don't understand what it's like, Ibby, you just don't! Like all bright and eager students, you think this field is about excavations, research and discovering the bloody truth. That's because you don't have the first idea of how things are really done. You don't … you …" Her voice trailed off.

I lowered my hands to see her gaping and pointing a trembling finger at the rings I still wore.

"Y-you brought them … 'here'?" She looked near panic, eyes wide and rolling.

"What the hell was I supposed to do with them?" My hands curled into fists. "I was also attacked this morning! It's not as though I've had time to develop a plan."

A loud gaggle of students passing outside the hall made us both jump and eye the exits.

"The plan," Schottelkirk said, hissing, "is to put those things back where you found them, and to play this off as a botched robbery. No discovery is worth this."

I wanted to argue with her, insist some things were indeed worth this kind of trouble, but one look in her eyes told me to save my breath. She was terrified, and I probably should have been the same. But something had changed in the alley, and I wasn't going to back down.

The answers I needed weren't going to be found here.

I looked at the photograph of Weston and Lowe, and a chill ran down my spine. I reconsidered. I was in the records building. Wasn't I?

I went to take Professor Schottelkirk's hands the way she had mine only last night, but she flinched away. Her eyes darted to the rings and then looked at me plaintively.

I squared my shoulders. "Take care of yourself, Professor," I said as gently as I could and then turned on my heel.

Schottelkirk didn't follow, only called after me as I moved towards the end of the hall that led into the records offices. "Where are you going? Damn it all, Ibby. What are you going to do?"

I didn't even look over my shoulder.

"LOWE? No, I'm sorry. There's no one on faculty under that name. I can tell you that right now."

Since finding the correction office in regards to faculty records, I'd been through two student volunteers and one junior administrative assistant, all as useful as a brolly in a hurricane. Now I stood before Yasmine, the undisputed matriarch of records — if the other staff's deference was any indication. A slight woman with dark, almond eyes and skin like beaten gold, probably nearing fifty by the streaks of grey in her otherwise immaculate hair, she surveyed her domain with absolute sovereignty.

And I, a vagabond in her little fiefdom, was quickly wearing out my welcome.

"I understand, ma'am." I put on bashful smile. "I was looking into a Professor Lowe that would have been in the faculty around the 1910s and into the 1920s, possibly. He was an expert in Near Eastern studies."

Yasmine narrowed her eyes, though whether in interest or suspicion I couldn't guess. She leaned forwards in her office chair, which squeaked, and she tapped her pen twice on the desk.

"Records that old would not be on our current system," she replied, eyes still narrowed. "We would have to search hard copies, which are in the basement … the sub-basement."

I felt the weight of her scrutiny, challenging me to make myself that much of a nuisance. As fierce a woman as Yasmine was, the rearrangement of my priorities since the attack left me more than a match for such obstacles. Still, there was no reason to be boorish about it. I cast my gaze lower and kept the sheepish smile.

"I'm sorry it's such a bother, but I would really appreciate it if we could look. I'm gathering sources on archaeology lecturers. It's for an essay on developing areas of focus, and Professor Lowe was referenced, but I really need some primary sources."

I looked up through my eyebrows and saw Yasmine watching me, unmoved.

"Please, ma'am? I'd be so grateful."

Yasmine raised one unnaturally defined eyebrow and seemed to make up her mind. Her desk drawer snapped open, she fished out an extensive collection of keys on a ring, and she popped up from her desk. "Let's make this quick, shall we?"

I tried to express my gratitude, but I was too busy trying to keep up with her.

The sub-basement of the records building was behind two locked doors and a flight of narrow stairs. On a small landing with a single sodium bulb shining over a steel security door, our little expedition nearly ended.

The door wasn't locked, but it was stuck. Yasmine threw her petite frame against it, pantsuit be damned, but it hardly budged. Trying not to show she was breathing hard, she replaced strands of hair that had escaped from her bun in the struggle. She looked at me tiredly. Her skin had turned a jaundiced shade in the overhead light.

"Could I have a go at it?" I asked, afraid she'd call the search off. I would have, if I were her.

"Be my guest," she shrugged and stepped back.

I was not as dainty as Yasmine, but no one had ever accused me of being particularly stout either. I stepped forwards. The steel of the door called out to me, a grinding, crotchety song. I laid my hands flat against the door, feeling my awareness expanding until I knew every warp and quirk. It was a strange, intimate sensation, almost frightening, but I recalled the construct of needle and thread. Steel was right where I could easily pluck its string. I gathered my will.

Open sesame.

A little bit went a long way, and the door flew open with ferocity. It hit the concrete wall inside with enough force to kick up dust. From within the dark corridor, the battered door gave a final protest on squealing hinges.

I looked back at Yasmine without having to fake another sheepish smile. "You must have loosened it for me."

"Quite," Yasmine squeaked, the tiny sound echoing up the stairs.

The blackness beyond was absolute, but my guide recovered and drew another key from her ring.

"Excuse me," she said softly, stepping lighter around me after my show of force. She reached just inside the door, and after a moment of fussing about, drove the key home and gave it a twist.

Hanging fluorescent lights came on one after another in a seemingly endless row. An annoying electric buzz filled the air. The sterile light revealed wire shelves flanking the narrow room where clear plastic bins sat stuffed with files.

"1910s to 1920s, you said?"

Yasmine led me in and pointed to laminated placards affixed to the shelves. Each placard was the size of a post-card and bore dates in bold black type.

"Yes, ma'am," I stepped into the room, noticing the subtle change in temperature. "Are these rooms climate controlled?"

Yasmine walked a few steps ahead of me, checking placards as she went. She didn't bother to look back or pause as she answered. "These records date back to the mid-19th century. They are as vital to our history as anything found in a museum and so require some extra care."

I let my new sense play over the documents in the bins.

With a little concentration, I could feel the staples and paperclips, each giving a little chime as I walked past.

"Here they are," Yasmine called, already in the process of dragging a bin off its shelf. She set the bin down and produced a pair of gloves. She drew out the first sheaf of documents from a thin plastic sleeve, and carefully parted a few leaves of the yellowed stationery.

"1920s," Yasmine murmured as though not wanting to disturb sleeping paper.

I found myself whispering, probably because she was doing it too, which I know sounds stupid. But it was contagious, especially as we were getting closer to discovering the truth.

"I assume 1920s, but the only date I'm sure about is 1918. He and Professor Weston, an Egyptologist, did some work together."

Yasmine gave me a wilting look. "That would have been helpful at the outset."

She replaced the documents and picked her way through the bin before coming up with a thin collection of papers. She flicked through several sheets — a collection of blunt typed text festooned with curls of handwritten script.

I hoped her intense glare indicated interest rather than frustration, but had to wait for a small eternity before she finally came up for air. She shook her head, and my heart dropped.

"Poor man," she intoned, her eyes bouncing back and forth over the documents. "I'm not sure you picked the right subject for your paper."

Her sad exclamation put my stomach in a knot and sparked an urge to shake the answers out of her. "Please," I said with forced calm. "Tell me everything."

"That's just it." A flutter of irritation plumed as she ran

a finger across an entry. "There is not that much here. Other than his association with Professor Weston, there isn't much to distinguish Professor Lowe."

Yasmine shook her head again, but eventually she began to read.

"Lowe, James Titus. Born 1866 in Bath, England. Came to the university at 17, studied philology and archaeology, specialising in Near Eastern cultures during the Bronze Age. Eventually, he became a fellow here and worked with the museum before becoming a lecturer and a full member of the faculty." She glanced up at me and back down at the page. "Looks as though the only thing of note he did was attend an excavation at the request of Professor Weston, where he identified some artefacts as being of Hittite provender, despite being located in Egypt. It was a minor discovery in 1918, but the First World War had just ended, and so archaeological news must have been scarce. Weston would go on to be one of those excavating the Valley of Kings in 1922, but for Lowe, that was it."

Here she looked up and gave me a quizzical look.

"Shouldn't you be doing your paper on Professor Weston? He seems a far more interesting subject. And shouldn't you be writing this down?"

In all the anxiety of finding the truth, I'd forgotten the number one rule of archaeology and scientific study in general: record everything.

"Please continue," I said after producing a pen and paper from my bag, both looking a little worse for wear after their recent abuses.

Yasmine gave another sigh, scanned a few lines and then began again.

"There's not much left, and none of it is good. After working with Weston in 1918 and completing an excavation in Palestine that — as far as it reads — produced no artefacts or discoveries of note, he lectured for two more years, with a note here saying 'sporadically.' By 1921, his evaluation of the work with Weston came under scrutiny and was eventually overturned, with several peers saying they were clearly Sumerian in origin and that Lowe's work was — in a word — 'shoddy.' There's no record of him making a defence, but it didn't matter, because at the turn of the year, 1922, he was found dead of an apparent heart attack outside his rooms at the university."

My vision blurred at the edges, and I put a hand on the nearest shelving unit to steady myself. I took a deep breath, willing myself not to faint. Yasmine didn't seem to notice my distress, thankfully.

"His services were paid for out of his modest estate with orders for cremation. Doesn't say what was done with the ashes, but I'm not surprised. Considering his relative disgrace, I'm surprised they kept this much. He wouldn't be the first scandal to be willingly forgotten."

Dead in 1922 from a heart attack. Cremated. All the moisture had vanished from my mouth. "Is there anything there about family? Children or a wife?" I rasped.

She shook her head. "No, it seemed Lowe died as unlucky in that regard as he did in his profession. Probably died of shame, the poor man. No one emerged to claim his estate." She shook her head with pity. "It's a true testament of loneliness when people don't even notice you enough to try and claim what you left behind. That's just a record keeper's editorial, mind you. Anyway, what was left was used to refurbish the faculty water closets in his old building. There's a rather rude handwritten note that says 'Lowe's Loos' in the margins, but I don't suppose that would be an honorific most would appreciate."

Dead, no family and with only a lavatory left behind.

It would have been funny if I hadn't actually met the

man only days ago. Both our careers had followed a path to the toilet, but I'd gotten there much faster.

Hittite, though … that couldn't be anything but intentional, especially with what I'd found within some Hittite pottery shards.

"Thank you." I slid my pen and paper back into my bag. "I appreciate you taking the time to help me like this."

Yasmine's head was still wagging as she put everything back into its rightful place.

"Well, it was diverting, at least. I'm sure you know what you are on about, but I'm telling you that Weston sounds a good deal more interesting than Lowe. Are you sure you're researching the right person?"

I recalled the tall, unsure man standing with me in Collections and how I'd been so scared he was a criminal or deviant. It was clear I should have been scared for an entirely different reason, even an impossible one.

Lowe was a ghost.

"No, ma'am," I said, demurely. "He's the right man."

Chapter Twelve

Sneaking back into the museum offices that afternoon was not nearly as clandestine as I first imagined.

Coming in the rear entrance, I was immediately spotted by Eddy, who looked half-asleep at his desk. Apparently, news of my scandal hadn't reached the porter, because he chatted about the most recent football matches — as usual — before waving me on.

That hurdle cleared, I headed down to Collections, hoping that the rubbish bins remained as badly neglected as they always were.

Collections was nearly abandoned. A single intern sat obediently at his workstation as I crept past, realising mid-creep such stealth wasn't necessary. The thumping beat of his hip-hop music could be heard through his earbuds, and he seemed far more interested in his phone than in any of the untouched boxes on the trolleys.

Where was Shelton when you actually needed him?

I swallowed a disgusted snort and made it to my station in short order. True to form, the rubbish bin sat untouched. Sitting on top was what I'd come for.

The bold type declaring the Grand Opening of the British Museum Station stared back at me as I grabbed the map and pocketed it. I wondered just how mad I had to be to consider this a serious option.

I should have gone to the nearest police station. Reported the attack, surrendered the rings and seen what kind of recovery could be made of my academic future. Archaeology might be out of the question, but maybe I could transfer to another department. I'd gotten high marks in the sciences, so why not examine my options on that score? Why couldn't I just go back to worrying about school and getting a good job?

I considered it as I slipped back into the elevator, but as the metal box enclosed me along with the humming of half a dozen metals and alloys, I knew the answer. I curled my fingers into a fist, feeling the rings.

You're not that girl anymore.

I stood in the elevator thinking of the million ways that this could all go bad and decided there was something I needed to do. It was probably mad, but that was the new norm. I pressed the button for Cataloguing. I didn't want to leave things as they were with Meredith. She was the closest thing I had to a real friend here, and I hated the idea of her thinking so little of me. I needed to talk to her. If nothing else, to say goodbye.

The doors opened as I slipped the rings off, figuring the conversation might go better if I wasn't still wearing them.

The call of the metals around me became more strident but less distinct. I'd been wearing the rings so long it took me off guard. I paused in the hallway to acclimatise to the burst of mental noise.

Peeking through the observation window to Lab D, I saw only the two knobheads, arguing.

"Bollocks," I said, hissing, then padded towards the small knot of offices in the centre of the floor.

Meredith avoided the offices like the plague, stating: "if I wanted to be in that rat race, I would have gone into business." But even she had to handle some administrative tasks.

I ran a greater risk of running into a staff member, but unless it was Shelton, I shouldn't have to put up with much aside from awkward stares. If Shelton did show up, I would have to fight the urge to pull one of the light fixtures down on his head.

Halfway there, it felt like I'd walked into a wall of metallic interference. I stumbled and would have fallen to one knee if I hadn't braced a hand on the wall. Steadied by the steel girder behind the plaster, I took several seconds to sort out the atonal blast bludgeoning my mind. I could barely think at first, but little by little, I understood what was afflicting me.

Metals, dozens upon dozens, possibly hundreds of different kinds, sent out overlapping ripples, each amplifying off of the others. The sheer number of angles staggered me, but the longer I endured, the more I could grasp the scope and complexity. Eyes closed, wincing, I began to discern the individual metals. The business of needles and string wasn't enough to describe this volume and variety. This was a tapestry. Instead of noticing individual strands, I took in the whole picture. These metals sat in orderly rows, rank upon rank like a metallic army.

I blinked up at the plastic sign fixed to the wall.

METALS CATALOGUE ROOM

"Oh, you've got to be joking," I gasped as a drop of sweat ran down the bridge of my nose.

No wonder I was doubled over. On the other side of the wall were hundreds of pure elements and alloys ranging the breadth of the periodic table. They were meant for comparison with artefacts and for stress tests.

It was an impressive collection and a Windsor-sized pain in my arse.

Shivering and doing my best to filter, I got to my feet. Human voices came through, talking in hoarse, half-whispers. The Metals room door was ajar …

"… that's entirely beside the point, Adrian," a woman's voice rasped. "Some of the junior staff heard what you said and are not happy about it."

Shelton's sanctimonious voice answered, "What are you on about? They should appreciate her being held accountable."

I took in a sharp breath.

"Young people love to debate what's fair," Meredith returned. "We were all puddin-headed plebes when we were young, even you. You know better than to make a scene like that."

Shelton sniffed, and I imagined him glaring down his nose at her.

"Don't you pull that rubbish with me, Adrian Shelton," she snarled. "I've been part of this circus as long as you have. When it comes down to it, you know I'm here to help you course correct."

There was a moment of silence and then a huff. Shelton spoke again but with a softer, more human voice.

"Yer right o' course, Mer," he admitted, a thick Scottish accent coming through. "Go on then, tell me what I buggered up this time."

I couldn't believe my ears. Shelton acting like a reasonable member of our species and Meredith collaborating with the enemy?

"Is it such a mystery?" she replied, her tone thick with sarcasm. "You just had to throw gender and skin colour into the mix. Didn't you?"

There was a stifled groan from Shelton. "Did I really do that?"

"You did! You daft, old ass!"

He had. The memory awakened a fresh fury in me. The rush of blood made my temples ache. I'd been so enraged by his bullying and belittling I'd never considered Shelton had targeted me for those factors. Shelton, the self-righteous brute, certainly. But Shelton, the racist misogynist, as well?

The thought of a modern-day scholar in authority using his position to execute such petty and vile prejudices made me sick with rage. Without thinking, I mentally squeezed the tapestry of metallic resonance. In response, each sample rocked as one in their containers. A dull rattle swept the room, silencing both speakers.

"What the devil was that?" Meredith gasped.

I squeezed my eyes shut in horror, realising what I'd done.

The silence stretched.

"Just the underground," Shelton said dismissively. There were footsteps, as though Shelton had begun pacing. "You're right, Meredith. I made a mistake," he continued in a lilt that I still struggled to associate with him. He must have worked very hard to cover it up if it was naturally that thick.

"That's putting it mildly," Meredith observed coolly. "Top brass gets word that you, a privileged white male, is throwing around bigoted language? They'll fire you on the spot. God knows, archaeology catches enough flak over you blokes."

Another sigh from Shelton, a low, defeated sound I

should have taken joy in. But all I heard was a man who was terribly weary. That was something I could and did sympathise with at least a little.

"Och, skelp me raw!" Shelton gave a muffled groan. "That wee scunner's boiled me proper!"

I didn't have a clue what he was saying, but felt my hackles rise. Who was he calling a 'scunner?'

"You're hard on all of them," Meredith cut in. "But why her? Why is it Ibby who gets you so topsy-turvy?"

Shelton didn't hesitate. "That harridan Schottelkirk's been nippin' at me since Bashir came, takin' turns threatenin' and flatterin'. Even before the daft rings, she had me runnin' scared. I s'pose I just took it out on the gel."

I frowned, wondering what Professor Schottelkirk had over Shelton, but imagining her harrying him perpetually over me was a new thought. Even with seeing her so brittle and fearful didn't change the fact that when she was in her element, she was an imposing woman. But he was still a racist woman-hater. Wasn't he?

"You could have Narissa come by …" Meredith began tentatively.

"No," Shelton snapped. "I'll no be using my wife like that."

"She'd gladly do it to save your job!"

"If my job is hangin' on the colour of my wife's skin, then ignorance has won, and I'm done anyway."

Okay, scratch the racist bit. What were the odds of misogyny sticking? Shelton was just a man with a temper and a tough job? That somehow seemed anticlimactic.

"Well," Meredith said, sighing. "At least you won before you went out."

"How d'you mean?" Shelton asked, sounding tired and very un-monstrous.

"While you were talking with those Metro bobbies,

Schottelkirk came by looking a fright. She said in no uncertain terms she was no longer Ibby's adviser. I'm not sure what happened, but the doors are shuttin' hard on that girl. Shame, really."

I never heard Shelton's reaction to the news.

The shock of Schottelkirk's betrayal was the proverbial straw to my overburdened camel. I closed my eyes and tilted my head back against the wall, my heart aching.

I needed to escape, needed space. With a heave, I pushed away from the wall. My mental grip on the tapestry slewed hard to the side. The metals room crashed with the sound of ingots slamming around inside of their containers. Some of them threw themselves onto the floor.

Meredith and Shelton's voices rose in cries of alarm, but I was already running for the exit.

MY FLAT WAS STILL in a state from earlier that morning, and with the dying sun painting everything red, it made quite the statement about domestic, urban decay. The spider-web crack on the window, shattered glass on the floor, the fork still in the love seat.

I choked back a sob.

Life as I knew it had come to an abrupt end, and I only barely understood why. In fact, the only thing that kept me upright and moving was the knowledge violent men were looking for me. I wanted to crumple onto my mattress and sleep through the next two terms.

Why think of time in terms? You aren't in school … not anymore.

Every pillar I'd built my life and future on seemed to be falling apart, and I was just trying not to get caught in the collapse. My mind raced, searching for something solid to hang on to. The old underground map came to mind. It wasn't a comfort or even much of a plan, but it was a direction.

Surveying my flat, I wondered what I should take on my little underground expedition.

Something wasn't right. After living here for a while, I'd become accustomed to the building's noises and patterns: the series of doors closing, steps upon the stairs as residents got off to work in the morning and the rumble from the basement in the evening while they did laundry.

I'd started to gather some clothes when I finally sussed it out — the footsteps on the stairs. This was the time of day when kids were back from school and raising an utter racket. There was no raucous noise, but there was the sound of heavy adult-sized steps from the stairwell.

A paranoid voice in my head asked: *If they could find you on the open street, why couldn't they find you here?*

My gaze swung back to the door where it hung slightly ajar, looking like it had been left open for company. 'Company' was nearly here. My arms prickled with the dread of it. They were coming for me.

Somewhere between here and Tottenham Court, I'd put the rings back on, and with a flick of my hand, the door swung shut. Control was still a crude thing, and it slammed. I winced, and the footsteps in the stairwell paused.

Rushing over, I bolted the door, not trusting myself to bolt it telepathically without tearing the bolt out of the wood.

Listening, my breathing uneven, my mind raced. The last time — even scared and ambushed — I'd managed to beat them. This time, I knew they were coming. Could I make a stand here?

Noises from the hallway sent a fresh dose of icy fear

into my spine: the sliding click of pistols, chambering a round. It was a sound I'd heard twice before, both times connected with a bad-news-boyfriend from my early teens. Even growing up in East End, guns represented a level of escalation most street toughs balked at. This was London, not New York or LA, where the media made it sound as though firearms grew on trees.

And it sounded like three of those rare murder devices were cocked, ready and waiting outside my flat.

I needed to get out. Now.

Desperately, I mentally pushed all the metal cast about my room and piled it in front of the door, willing it to stay. I hoped it held like the little pot because that, at least, would buy me time. I moved to the bathroom and locked the door before heading to the small window.

I thought I could hear them coming down the hall as I forced the window open, using my power to get the metal to cooperate. The thick glass sported several jagged cracks as the metal twisted to my will.

A knock sounded at my door, and my heart jackhammered in response. If they started shooting, the thin interior walls wouldn't be much protection.

It was a tight fit, but I managed to get a leg, my head and shoulders out the window when I heard thuds against the door, which could only mean they were trying to break the door down. There were muffled curses. I assumed the magnetised pile of metal was holding.

Small comfort that was as I looked down from five stories up.

With one leg dangling, I closed my eyes briefly to calm a wave of vertigo. If I had underestimated my new powers, I wouldn't have to worry about the guns.

The pitted concrete exterior of my building didn't offer any helpful ledge or shelf, but the brick structure across the alleyway was festooned with pipes. Blocking out the sound of a body throwing itself against my barricaded door, I eyed a pipe running from ground level and over the top of the building.

I bid the aluminium alloy to come to me. There was a squeal of protest from the metal bands that mounted it against the side of the wall, but they came free with little puffs of brick dust. Like a fakir's trick, the pipe swayed towards me. It spanned the narrow alleyway, but sections of it began to slide and separate as it tilted closer. My consciousness ran the length of the pipe, reinforcing it.

"Hold together now," I hissed the words through gritted teeth.

I heard the thugs in the hallway talking. Then a burst of silenced gunfire tore through my flat. I stifled a scream as a bullet punched through my living room window and struck the brick building opposite.

Time's up.

Grasping the pipe with a trembling hand, I hauled myself out the window, barking my shin on the sill. My stomach swayed sickly as I wrapped myself around the pipe and tried not to look down.

Guiding the pipe downwards and throwing my whole mind into reinforcing it, I came two storeys closer to the ground before registering pain in my hands. The metal was unpleasantly warm. As the pain intensified, my focus slipped. My body jerked and bounced as the pipe began to buckle.

Lurching another storey lower, I nearly lost my grip before I managed to reassert control. The pipe bobbed and creaked as my mind gripped it. Breathing hard, I stilled the metal and braved a look down. Just a little lower, and I could drop to the ground without breaking any bones.

Another burst of gunfire sounded overhead, longer this

time and somehow angrier. The mounting pain in my hands and the pistol-fire divided my attention again. The pipe buckled further. My stomach gave a sick lurch. Screaming, I swung towards the bricks.

I twisted around the pipe, and with a grunt, took the brunt of the impact on my left shoulder. Pain shot along my collarbone, and I hissed, tightening my poor hands around the pipe. My arms and shoulders quivered with fatigue. My hands were two points of agony, and my whole left side throbbed, but I hadn't lost my grip.

Touchdown came a few agonising, seemingly eternal seconds later. Relieved, I released the pipe and crouched on the alley floor. Metal squealed and squeaked as the twisted pipe dangled overhead. Beyond the pipe, I heard a splintery crunch. Bolting down the alley like a sprinter out of the blocks, I careered towards the front of the building.

I slid to a stop at the corner and pressed against the wall as a thought struck.

What if they'd left someone outside, waiting to grab me if I tried to escape?

All of my painful antics with the pipe would have been in vain. Shrinking against the brick and half-expecting gunshots, I peeked around the corner.

The sidewalk in front of the complex held only the usual traffic. The gunfire from my flat would have been too muffled for anyone to have noticed. People went about their business. The way appeared absent of a lurking ruffian.

I was about to slip into the street nonchalantly when I spotted something out of the ordinary. Across the road, just out of the way of those walking by, a darkly dressed figure stared at his phone intently.

He was dressed too nicely for my neighbourhood. His coat and slacks were sleek and expensive looking, and if those rings on his hands were real, they could have paid my rent for a year. More than that, he looked too … too pretty, too put together for the typical blokes in my area. But he was familiar in a way I couldn't define.

Then he looked up from his phone.

There was the perpetual shrug, the dark brow on a startlingly handsome face. Dillon, Jackie's mon chou, stood watching my building.

Gaping, I ducked in behind a passing knot of teenagers, who didn't notice the little hitchhiker who crept in close behind them. My mind spun.

Why would Dillon be standing outside my flat at the exact time armed thugs were storming in? Why would Jackie's boyfriend be waiting outside a building in a neighbourhood he clearly didn't belong in? According to Jackie, he was tied to the university and was plugged in — through one connection or another — to the faculty in the archaeology department.

A terrible suspicion — blooming into something resembling a conspiracy — took shape in my mind as I pressed as close to my concealing patch of humanity as I dared. The troupe of youths rounded a corner, and I threw a look over my shoulder. Dillon was talking on the phone now. Judging from his body language, he was unhappy, bordering on angry. He looked ready to hurl the phone across the street as he glared up at my building.

Sirens sounded in the distance, and Dillon's whole body tightened as he hung up. Sliding his phone into his coat pocket, he put a good deal of effort into casually strolling down the street. I lost sight of him as I rounded the corner.

Just because I was paranoid didn't mean I was wrong.

Regardless, I found myself now not only jobless and

futureless but without a home. All I had was what was in my bag, my phone and the rings.

The police would have questions about why anyone would shoot up my apartment, and I didn't have answers. Dots would be connected, and I could expect to find the rings confiscated and myself locked in a cell.

I got out my phone and sent a text to Jackie as fast as my fingers could manage.

Hey luv, cnt explain, but pls stay away frm Dillon. <3 call soon, be sfe

If I was lucky, she'd wait to talk to me before she met with Dillon again.

In the meantime, I needed answers, and there was only one place I might find them. I fished out the old map and headed for the tube.

Chapter Thirteen

Calling myself insane more than once, I descended into Covent Garden Station. The rush of people eased as the hour grew late. It had been early evening when I'd fled, and it was nearing eight o'clock. Second-guessing myself and dithering resulted in a dawdling pace. I'd grabbed a wrap for dinner and sat chewing and stewing, trying to come up with a better plan than chasing ghosts.

I was an archaeologist-adjacent after all, not some daft, mumbling spiritualist. Yet, here I was on a foggy London evening, trotting into the underground looking to find a ghost.

But not the one everyone else was looking for.

Covent Garden is one of the most famous haunted stations in London. Supposedly, the ghost of an actor might be seen moving about the station at night, standing on the platforms and looking a proper English ghost. As such, there were sometimes teams of amateur ghost hunters, bored youngsters and the occasional meandering herd of spook tourists following a guide in garish attire.

I skirted past a group of teens taking selfies and making

ghastly faces. I realised with a jar it had only been a few years since I was their age. I stifled a surge of jealousy.

What right did they have to be so happy, so carefree? One look told me they knew nothing of hardship. They were equipped with the latest phones and clothing that cost as much as the security deposit on my flat. Speaking of which, I wasn't getting it back.

They were born into an affluence I would never have.

The answering voice sent a chill down my spine: *Make it better by being better.*

I went further down the platform, away from the teens, towards the quiet end … and a maintenance door. Drawing out the map, I checked the way the lines intersected. Covent Garden was a straight shot to Museum Station. The only way of getting to the defunct station would be through the maintenance corridors.

I steeled myself to pop the door open, looking out for station staff or anyone watching me. I'd have to use my power.

The approaching rumble of a train made me smile and put a hand on the door. The arrival of the train would provide the perfect cover as I broke the lock.

Then I heard a steam engine whistle.

I straightened, confused. The subways hadn't run steam engines since WWI. It had to be a gimmick. Maybe the station was celebrating some … anniversary …

My eyes widened as a vintage train rolled to a stop beside me. The doors slid open.

Painted wood panelling framed an entry into an empty carriage. The seats were forward-facing benches complete with elegant legs. There was a faint air of tobacco smoke and old grease, but it looked like an Edwardian sitting room, not a modern tube cabin. No slick plastics, no bright primary colours or tacky upholstery.

A tourist attraction cabin then. A historic piece meant to give a scenic tour of the underground.

I looked down the platform to check my hypothesis, expecting to see a tour mob rushing for the door. What I saw instead was far worse.

I was alone.

There was no one else here, or if they were here, I couldn't see them. It was as though the crowds had simply seeped away, into another realm. My jaw went slack, and my mouth dried as my gaze slid from the abandoned platform to the patiently waiting carriage.

Ghost carriage.

Was I really going to trust this phantom train? How did I know I wouldn't pitch headfirst onto the rails when I took a step? I turned to my new sense and felt the metals of the carriage, the bolts in the floor, the ribbed girders giving it shape. It was what I needed to finally take that fateful step.

I walked into the carriage and took a deep breath as the doors closed behind me. Sinking onto the nearest bench, my hands braced the edge, feeling its sturdiness.

With a great hiss and some heavy chugging, the train lurched into the darkness of the underground.

There were no glaring overhead lights, only a smattering of softly glowing lamps, inviting me to relax. The ambience of the carriage, the steady rocking, the absence of the usual crowds. Exhaustion settled over me. My feet throbbed and eyes burned. I let my eyelids droop shut. Despair threatened to swamp me.

"Miss Bashir?"

I'd fallen asleep … was dreaming …

"I'm terribly sorry, madame."

My eyes flew open, and I sprang to my feet, dazed.

"I wish I could let you sleep, but I am afraid we are rather pressed for time."

Standing at the open carriage door, his silver head poking in, was Professor Lowe.

"What are you?"

The words came out a brusque question, perhaps more abrupt than I had intended, and I was surprised when Lowe looked at me with apparent hurt.

"Madame, I think you mean who am I. Asking what I am, besides being quite rude, implies we are not peers or even the same species. Still, I would ask that you disembark, and we can discuss this further."

I shook my head. "You're either a one-hundred-and-fifty year old man who faked his death, or you're a ghost."

Lowe frowned, anxious for me to get out of the car but hesitant to come and get me. He looked up and down the length of the train, then steepled his fingers.

"Very well, if I answer your question, will you step out? The train will be leaving soon, and I'm not certain I can join you."

Interesting. "Depends on your answer." I crossed my arms.

Lowe's pale eyes darted the length of the carriage again, but he nodded. "Yes, my corporeal existence ended some time ago. Laxity and the passage of time can dull the intellect and obfuscate memories, but I have been waiting for a very long time."

"What for?"

Lowe met my gaze. Potent emotions warred in his typically mild expression. Pride, sadness and even paternal affection.

"Why, for you, my dear." He lifted a hand, palm up.

Slowly, I put my hand in his and stepped onto the platform.

"I'm glad to see my warning had the desired effect." Lowe smiled, eyeing the rings on my hands.

The statement filled me with a tremor of trepidation as the doors closed behind me and the train rolled off into the dark.

"WELCOME TO MUSEUM STATION," Lowe said warmly as he led me from the spiral staircase we'd taken up from the platform below.

I'd seen photographs of the old British Museum Station, and this was nothing like that crumbling death-trap. The real Museum Station had been shut down in 1933, then slowly picked apart. Stripped down and demolished over the decades until only the bones were left.

Where we stood now was a turn of the century underground station, but with antique decorations in a pseudo-Egyptian motif. The posts flanking the stairwell were shaped like smooth stone columns, and the tiled walls were painted to resemble the reed-lined Nile.

"Sorry, but where am I?"

"Ms Bashir," Lowe said patiently, templing his fingers in that way he had. "As the pamphlet states, you are at the British Museum Station."

"Except, not," I said, looking around at the softly lit sconces shaped like pyramids. "I looked it up. The real station was demolished. This can't be it."

Lowe stretched his arms wide. "You can see me, can even touch me and yet the 'real' me is a pile of ash and bone fragments sitting in an urn somewhere. The station — like myself — has left behind its corporeal existence and now operates in a different reality."

We crossed a wide lobby-like space as he said this.

Two broad stairwells in opposite corners boasted

signage proclaiming they led up to the museum exhibit floors.

"A ghost station …" I murmured, gazing around. We'd stopped in the large waiting area with benches around a central courtyard, flanked by concrete pillars with an understated connection to Ancient Egypt. In the centre was an obelisk, whose dark surface was etched in hieroglyphics inlaid with gilt paint.

"I prefer the poetry of alliteration," Lowe said, slightly flamboyantly, "so I would call it a spectral station, but I am not opposed to you calling it whatever takes your fancy."

Lowe gestured to the benches, and we crossed the polished floor.

"That really doesn't tell me where I am, at least spatially," I said, sinking onto a padded bench. "Are we under the station, alongside the station in some alternate reality? In the same place just in a different realm? Or, am I hallucinating?"

The possibility this was a figment of my stressed imagination didn't bother me anymore. A wave of weariness fell over me. My shoulder and neck ached from where I'd struck the wall, and my hands were still sensitive from the hot pipe. I wondered if Lowe would mind if I lay down on the bench. I was past being picky about where I dozed.

Lowe looked as perky as I was exhausted. He sat beside me, spine ramrod straight. "You are familiar with the theory called the Law of Conservation of Matter, yes?"

I nodded.

"Very good. It states that because my body — my matter — is otherwise occupied in that ghastly urn, I should not be here interacting with you. After all, matter is neither created nor destroyed, yet I am here and just as solid as ever I was. Even able to take your hand. But it is not always so. Thus, I am a manifestation of a kind of energy, psychic perhaps, able to interact with the material world along structures I barely understand. I believe this station manifests in a similar way."

Lowe's eyes sank to the floor, and his posture wilted. His next words were soft.

"Despite all the time spent being deceased, there is a great deal about my current condition that I understand only by intuition."

"Why didn't you just come out and tell me?" I asked. "Why go through this charade?"

"Were you likely to take me seriously if I had been forthright?" Lowe asked with a wry grin. "Honestly."

I didn't answer. We both knew how I would have reacted.

"You said you've been waiting," I began. "… for me, and I assume these." I held up the rings and studied his face for a reaction. For a dead guy, Lowe wore his dead but sincere heart on his sleeve.

His gaze settled on the rings, his expression managing to be both affectionate and dubious at the same time. "You and those and so much more."

I shouldn't have been surprised. In a few days, these rings had turned my life upside down. Now I was talking to a ghost who was somehow connected to them. I imagined his relationship with them might be … complex.

"Are you talking about the powers they gave me?"

"Yes," he began and then shivered as though experiencing a sudden chill. "No. That is to say, the rings did not give you your powers."

I gave him a quizzical look. "Yes, they did."

His dour expression broke into a small, satisfied smile. "Did you have anyone else attempt to use the rings?"

I blinked. As a matter of fact, I hadn't, but that was

because I'd been perpetually trying to hide my theft. I expressed as much, and the smirk widened into a grin.

"Had you attempted it, you would have been frustrated at every turn, much as I was. Though the rings may have acted as a catalyst for your bloodline's expression, one without the proper parentage would have had no such luck. To them, it would be a gaudy broken gauntlet, nothing more."

I looked at the rings, and felt an irrational defensiveness over whether the rings were in fact 'gaudy.' Perhaps too chunky to be elegant, but a girl could appreciate something with some heft to it … wait … I dragged my gaze from the rings.

"Bloodline?"

Lowe watched me with a mix of concern and curiosity. "You are feeling the pull of the rings, aren't you?"

I crossed my arms and hid the rings in my armpit. He was right. I was having a hard time not looking at them. They were the only things that seemed solid at the moment.

Ghosts, bloodlines and rings that wake up super powers. I was in desperate need of contextual information.

"You first."

Lowe turned to face me, both hands resting on his knees. A twinkle came into his eyes.

"As a student of archaeology, you know events and people do not emerge from a vacuum. People emerge from families, communities and cultures, which have shaped them before their birth. In you, Ms Bashir, we see people and events coalescing into a single body. Your birth was what our people have been waiting for."

"'Our' people?" I cocked a sardonic eyebrow.

His spirit fired, Lowe sprang to his feet and began to pace and gesture. A lecturer without a class for nearly a century. He was in his element; he had an audience. I had a fleeting moment of fear at what I'd unleashed. But Lowe, for all his social awkwardness and spectral ticks, was a superb storyteller.

"There's no need to stare at your skin or mine," he said with enthusiasm. "Whatever ethnic heritage that we descend from, we are part of a lineage that dates back to the cradle of human civilisation, to the very banks of the Euphrates and ziggurats of Sumer." He held up an authoritative finger. "Where early man mined his first ores. Where our people — the *Inconquo* — began."

Inconquo. The word echoed in my mind, shivered through my veins.

"They sprang up in the days when mankind was learning he could shape the world with his will and mind. From one of the greatest minds and wills came our ancestors, who had learned the secret tongues of metals and thus commanded them. Our first fathers and mothers were alchemists and magi, speaking to the metals, learning their secrets and bending them to serve man. It is no exaggeration that the marvels of the ancient world stand as testament to the effect of the Inconquo, but for all that, being mystic scholars and craftsmen was not their most vital function."

He hesitated, playing the pregnant pause as though he were a master violinist playing the silence between notes. He caught my gaze with his own, his eyes soft.

"They were guardians."

I leaned forwards, skin prickling, something in me rising up. Guardians? I felt a vague sense of falling. It felt familiar, from dreams I couldn't remember. I tasted something burned and ashen in the back of my throat.

"Vigilant sentinels," Lowe continued, "they guarded mankind against threats, which today are dismissed to the annals of mythology. The stories are considered fanciful because of the Inconquo's service. We drove out those beings who would have kept mankind hiding in caves. Monsters, demons, though not strictly the sort in the Judaeo-Christian tradition. But all were powerful and dangerous. These terrible beings, many of them worshipped as gods by the ignorant and fearful, were our foes, and the rings were made to defeat such false gods."

I started as he took a long step towards me, my mind so divided between listening to him and trying to ignore the gritty dryness threatening to choke me. Quickly but not without care, he reached down, took my hand and held up the rings between us. I flinched at how cold his fingers felt. I hadn't realised my skin had become so flushed, almost feverish.

"These two rings are part of a set of four that when complete are the ultimate weapon against evil. Our ancestors poured themselves into their forging. That is why you are drawn to them, and why my spirit is bound to them. They are part of us."

The way he looked at them made me wonder if he felt the same, but the thought was washed away by a taste like scorched bread and dust, rising like gorge in my oesophagus. I tried to speak, but was only partially successful, and even then, my voice was a tight rasp.

"Is that why I'm having nightmares?"

Lowe's bright expression faltered as he bent over the rings. Behind his spectacles, his eyes darted, first to the metal on my fingers and then to my face.

"Nightmares?"

I tried to speak but coughed instead, my mouth filling with that awful taste. I swallowed and it was like eating gravel, but I managed to croak out a few words. "There was ash … and cinders …"

I covered my mouth as a cough wracked me. My eyes watered, and my lungs screamed for air. The hand at my mouth felt powdery, as though I'd been sifting fine soil. Holding my palm up, through bleary vision, I saw it was caked with ashes.

Lowe hissed and stood abruptly, his eyes alight. "*Kezsarak*!"

"What?" I gasped and then put my head between my knees as another barking attack of coughs seized me.

Ash, in thick black puffs, came out with every retch. My lungs clenched in a desperate cry for air. A small, sooty drift formed in front of my face and seemed to swell. I realised dreamily the drift wasn't swelling. I was falling, just before I ploughed face first into the floor.

Chapter Fourteen

The darkness around me was not absolute, but how I wished it were.

Dim, guttering images flared with sullen light, great grinding expanses of gears looming over me, inching closer with each flare. The light came with belches of heat, scalding air pricking at the nose with sulphurous breath. I could barely breathe. Crawling on my hands and knees over the fire-blackened floor, my palms were gouged, and my fingers scraped by spurs of metal and hunks of ore.

I had to get out, had to escape, but every creeping movement away from the gears told me I was only delaying the inevitable. The gears were getting closer, and all my scrambling hadn't bought me any time. I watched in horror as the cogs were backlit in a red, hellish light. The first tine of the machine grabbed me and dragged me under.

Incredible pressure worked its way over me. It paired with a heat that set my hair and clothes to smoking. There was pain, but I surrendered to it, thinking that if I just let it take me, then things would end. I would be crushed, scorched, ground into smoking dust, but at least it would be over.

But the great grinding ceased with heavy clanks and the screech of tortured metal. I still could not see as the glow had died, but I could feel the bite of the gears in my flesh and between my bones. Broken and trapped. A terrible claustrophobic panic filled me.

How long would I lie here, gumming up the works of this terrible engine? I began to wrench and squirm. The unforgiving gears held me fast. It was agonising, exhausting.

My panting breath was the only sound as I managed to get an arm free. Something rumbled in the darkness.

Using my free hand — which was thankfully and *unexpectedly whole — I leveraged more force, dragging more of my body free from the machine.*

In front of my face came a whistling blast of noxious steam, spattering my skin with little caustic dots.

SQUIRM.

It was the roaring voice, but the thunderous bellow was gone, replaced by an insidious, bubbling hiss.

SQUIRM AND WRITHE.

I cursed and panted as I fought to free myself. More gouts erupted around me, streaking my skin with tracks of burning liquid. I screamed but kept fighting, fixed on freeing myself, inch by painful inch.

WRITHE FAITHLESS, WRITHE WORM, WRITHE AND HOPE.

I'd worked my other arm free with a wet pop, but again — impossibly — it worked well enough that I was driving both my hands against the notches and grooves trapping my body from the chest down. I gasped for a fuller breath as, little by little, my ribs came free and expanded. Beautiful, blessed air filled me. In spite of the taunting voice, I began to think I might get free. It would hurt, but I could do it.

I was doing it!

More jets of steam burned my skin.

HOPE.

The word hung in the air, sliding between the searing shower.

HOPE, THAT I MAY TAKE MORE FROM YOU.

Like a switch was flipped, the darkness was filled with blazing light, radiating from the gears and wringing fresh agony. The gears began to turn anew, scraping and screeching to life. I heard my bones cracking and popping as it drew me back in.

I screamed and fought, but it was useless. I was being fed back to the cramped, broken dark. Back to the agony of a deathless imprisonment.

I sobbed a wordless, animal plea as I was sucked out of the furnace light. The voice filled the darkness with a thick, liquid laugh.

I SHOT UP, trying to scream, but my body was so tight with fear I didn't have the air for it. What passed my lips was a high-pressure whine.

"Steady on. It's all right. You are all right."

But I'm not! I'm dying, being crushed …

The world came into focus.

Lowe knelt beside me. In spite of kneeling in a ring of soot, his apparel remained clean. I was not so lucky. My clothing was caked with the stuff. I didn't care. The relief at seeing my arms and legs intact was so immense, it swallowed all other concerns. Looking down to see my chest rising and falling, unrestricted beneath my stained blouse was an utter thrill.

A dream. It had been nothing but a terrible dream.

"That a girl." Lowe's cool hand was braced against my sweaty forehead.

I collapsed bonelessly onto a mound of ash with a groan.

"That seemed wholly unpleasant," Lowe observed as he shifted back onto his haunches. "How are you feeling?"

I was enjoying unrestricted breathing too much to waste air on words, but threw up an a-okay hand gesture.

Come to think of it, my muscles felt weak, my stomach empty. And what I would do for a glass of water or seven!

Gingerly, I placed my hands against my ribs and savoured the expansion of each breath.

Lowe squatted next to me, watching to see if I was about to start spewing soot again, then got to his feet. He straightened his coat and adjusted his spectacles, before reaching down to help me up.

"I'm afraid you must get up, Ms Bashir. There is still so much more to do."

"Call me, Ibby," I said with a trembling voice, looking up at him without budging. "And I think I'll just stay here for a bit, you know. Rest my eyes."

Lowe gave me a sad smile. "You've been resting your eyes for the better part of two days."

My jaw dropped. "You let me sleep for two days?"

Lowe nodded gravely and waggled his hand in front of me. With a grumble of some less than genteel phrasing, I let him haul me to my feet.

"I don't believe 'let you sleep' is the correct way to describe the situation. You collapsed, and I watched over you since you could not be wakened. I wasn't sure you would recover and might join me here as a permanent resident."

I was in a coma for two days, and he was making jokes? Two days! My mind boggled.

"You couldn't have called for help? You might be fine with being a ghost, but that doesn't mean I want to bloody well join you!"

A flicker of hurt raced across Lowe's face, and I felt a sharp sting of guilt. Bad enough I was criticising him, but worse, I was hurling his condition back in his face. It was an unworthy thing to do. Before I could apologise, he turned and gestured to an end table where a pitcher and glass sat.

"Are you thirsty?"

My throat tightened. "Very."

In the small room, the table was positioned next to an old upright radio, while against the far wall, a typewriter sat on a roll-top desk.

Lowe poured a glass and handed it to me. The water was cool with a hint of citrus. The feeling of it upon my dusty throat was a heavenly, soothing nectar. I greedily gulped it down.

Lowe stood by patiently, and once I'd drained the glass, he offered to fill it again.

I panted, holding it out.

"I'm sorry if it seems my actions were callous to your state," Lowe said as he filled my glass. "But there is no modern medicine which would have helped."

I drank the second glass more slowly.

"I don't suppose many hospitals get patients spontaneously coughing up ash," I allowed, then shuddered at the memory as I looked at the floor where I'd woken. Nearly two inches of soot caked the ground, drifting several inches higher in some places. "Sorry about the mess."

Lowe chuckled. "It's no bother. The station has already disposed of the bulk of what your body expelled. I imagine, before tomorrow, this will be gone as well."

He replaced the pitcher and gestured to the door behind me. "Perhaps we should return to more spacious environs to finish our conversation?"

I nodded but reached over and grabbed the pitcher. "I'm bringing this."

"Very good." Lowe led me through the doorway to a small corridor with wooden floors and oak panelled walls. At the end of this short passageway was an ovoid door with a crank wheel in its centre. Lowe spun the wheel, and the portal slid open a few inches, allowing the ghost to draw it open. He gestured for me to pass into the commons, where we'd been sitting before I'd had the ash episode.

My gaze swept the area, expecting to see dark smears on the ground, but the polished concrete floor was gleaming.

"You said that the station had disposed of the ashes. Does that mean that it is … animate?"

The door closed with a heavy thump, and Lowe spun the wheel.

"In the time I've been here, a certain level of status quo has been maintained. Refuse and rubbish are cleaned while furniture reorients itself to original configurations."

"I could use a room down here," I murmured and took another sip of water.

Lowe walked past me towards the central arrangement of pillars. "Come. Your things are this way."

At the foot of the obelisk centring the courtyard was my bag, and next to it, my phone. Lowe levelled a finger at the latter and frowned.

"That little device has been giving signals over the time that you were unconscious. I placed it here to spare both of us its complaints."

I knelt, putting down the pitcher and cup. Picking up the phone, I was greeted by a black, lifeless screen. The battery was dead of course. Two days without a charge and a day's worth of use before I took my sooty little nap. I slipped the phone into my bag then shouldered it before snatching up the glass of water.

"Okay." I turned back to Lowe. "Lay it on me. Why am I having nightmares and coughing up ash?" I recalled the word he'd hissed at the moment of my coughing fit. "What is a Kezsarak?"

Lowe nodded. "Kezsarak is a demon, a *gallu*, as the ancient Sumerians called them. He is the reason for your nightmares and the ectoplasmic attacks. They are his opening salvo now that he is aware of you."

"Ectoplasmic?"

Lowe bobbed his head. "The connection between you and the demon will grow stronger. He will use the foothold gained through your nightmares to make your life … uncomfortable."

A day ago … wait, damn it … well, a few days ago, I didn't believe in demons, ghosts or magical bloodlines. Now I found myself in a phantom tube station, listening to a ghost. A ghost from a magic bloodline I was part of as he told me about a demon that was after me. I wanted to be sceptical but having soot pour from my lungs made it difficult. One mad explanation seemed as good as any other, at this juncture.

"What's his beef?"

Lowe frowned. "I beg your pardon?"

"Why would this gallu want to come after me? Because I'm an Inconquo?" Whatever that was.

Lowe crossed his arms, trying and failing to hide another one of those weird shivers. The ghost was quirky. I'd give him that.

"From my understanding, which is purely academic, gallu do not need a reason for making trouble. This particular one is very old with a tragic history. The most important thing to know is that while his attacks on you are uncomfortable and disruptive, they cannot be lethal. But if he escapes, he won't bother harassing your mind. He will simply find you and kill you."

While I would describe the most recent attack as a bit

more than uncomfortable, I tried to focus on the 'kill you' part. Priorities and all.

"You say 'if' he escapes, but you also say that he is getting closer. Closer in some metaphysical sense?" I was getting the hang of things.

Lowe nodded. "I understand your confusion. No, Kezsarak is contained within some kind of vessel. Again, my understanding is …"

"Academic, yeah. I got that part."

"Very good." Lowe frowned and then pinched the bridge of his nose. "So yes, he was imprisoned in this vessel by an Inconquo sometime around the 10th century BC. Yet, I have every reason to believe that said vessel is in the possession of the same organisation who was responsible for my death when I refused to assist them. Now that those," he nodded at the two rings on my hand, "have resurfaced, they are moving the vessel to London in the hopes of using the rings to open it."

The statement was a real one-two blow that left me wishing I could go back and lie on the floor of Lowe's office. First, it confirmed my adversaries weren't just opportunistic antiquity thieves but perhaps part of a larger conspiracy. Second, they weren't squeamish about people's lives. That would explain why everything moved so fast. This organisation must have been lying in wait for just such an opportunity. When Schottelkirk started circulating news about the rings, they pounced.

"What do they want to open the vessel for?"

Lowe held up his hands and shook his head. "I haven't the foggiest, but I can't imagine they have honourable intentions. This group murders people who refuse to join them."

I nodded. "Or send thugs to attack a girl in an alleyway."

Lowe's eyes widened a little and the venerable lines in his face deepened. "How dreadful. I'm so sorry, my dear."

I shrugged and suppressed a shiver as memories of the encounter played through my head. It was perverse how such powerful emotions occupied the same memory. Alongside the terror of that knife flashing in front of me, there was the exhilaration of watching them flee.

"It's all right, really." I mused. "They didn't expect me to use the rings, and that helped drive them off. I think they are even more in the dark about my powers than we are. When they showed up with guns, it was the rings that saved my life."

That strange frustrated look rippled over Lowe's features again, just before being replaced by another resigned look. "I'm sorry you've had to endure this, Ibby. I truly am, but I believe we've only scratched the surface of what they are capable of. Some of them may be ignorant, but not all. You will have to be very careful when you are out there tonight."

That brought me up short. Despite the surreality of staying in a ghost station, it was currently the safest option in London.

"Tonight? Why tonight? We did just cover the fact that there is a pack of homicidal maniacs looking for the rings. Doesn't going out there play into their hands?"

"That might be the case, but the reality is that we only have half the rings. Before my death, I found the complete set. Fearing the worst, I broke the rings in half, and I hid one half in the museum and the other in my office at the university. You found the ones in the museum, but the half in my office is still at risk. You need to get them."

"Why do 'I' have to go? You're the ghost, aren't you? It's not like they can kill you again. And who is this 'they,' anyway?" The words were barely out and I felt ashamed.

"Lowe … James, I'm sorry that was rude, and cowardly … and …"

Lowe reached out and took my hand, giving my fingers a soft squeeze before withdrawing.

"Ibby, it's all right. The simple answer is that I can't. You have no idea how many times I've wished I could do more, but there are limits imposed on me by this incorporeal state. Just as you seem to be the only one that can see me, the rings are among those items which I cannot interact with. Further, in death I can only travel to the places I visited most in my life. I am in so many ways a prisoner of this unlife."

I struggled to meet his eyes, and I was thankful when he cleared his throat and gestured towards the spiral staircase leading to the rail platform below.

"As to who these people are, I am not certain, but when they attempted to induct me, they indicated that they were an old and powerful society. The fact that they were able to react so quickly to the revelation of the rings seems to imply they weren't lying."

"How do we even know they are the same group?" I asked, adjusting my bag.

"Kezsarak's presence seems good evidence. They hinted they could give me access to one of the Inconquo's oldest enemies. Kezsarak is the only entity I know of whom they imprisoned rather than destroyed." Lowe reached the stairs first and turned to me. "After you, madame."

The stairs yawned in front of me, a reminder that once I went down, that phantom train would arrive to sweep me into a world of fear and danger. All of that risk for what? To stop some crusty old circle of maniacs from unleashing one more blight on mankind? Would anybody even notice? When was the last time the human race saw fit to look out for me? Why did it have to be me, Ibukun Bashir, to carry this?

Make it better by being better.

With Lowe standing there, arm outstretched to usher me to the platform, I hated my father's words. Hated their truth, their weight, their burden. I didn't want to make it better. I wanted it to be better for me, and I didn't care how selfish that was. For a moment, I rejected everything my parents taught me, everything I knew, everything I believed.

Then that moment passed.

I allowed myself one more deep breath before marching down those stairs and onto the ghost train.

Chapter Fifteen

Night was falling as I arrived at Covent Garden, but if I was going to sneak onto university grounds, I was going to have to wait a bit. Loitering around campus itself wasn't advisable, and besides that, I needed to sort a few things out.

First, was wardrobe.

A thrift shop near the station called Rokit seemed the best place to take my sooty self. I had a little money, enough to get some dark jeans and a black tank top. It had a garish, paint-spattered Union Jack, and it was hard to tell if the jeans were distressed or just badly worn, but at least, I was able to shed the ash-streaked clothes. Nipping into the loo before dressing, I did my best to scrub the ash from my body. Nearly three days without a shower, not to mention an afternoon running for my life, had left me in quite a state.

As scrubbed and polished as I could be, I trotted down to Monmouth Coffee. The place was heaving with customers, but the press of people made me feel safer. I hoped this group wouldn't dare come after me with twenty witnesses in shouting distance.

I sat at one of the back tables, my phone plugged into the wall, watching the people shuffle in line to get coffee and a pastry. There wasn't much seating so most would either take away or hang about outside, where a few benches sat against the building. Sometimes, I thought one of the patrons was paying too much attention to me, but when I looked away or gave a slight nod of my head, they all moved on.

All except the one standing in front of me now.

Lanky but for a thick neck and round face, he was not classically handsome, but he got full marks for determination.

"So, you come here often?" he asked as he took a sip of his latte.

Looking bored, I gazed past him. "Just needed a charge." I gestured absently at my phone and craned my neck, not appreciating how he was blocking my view of the shop and the street.

"Yeah, isn't that just the worst," he said, chuckling, then took another sip before his eyes brightened. "Hey, if you need to use my phone, it's no problem." He began to dig into his trouser pocket.

I shook my head and waved him off. "Thank you, though."

He smiled, somehow taking my gracious manner for interest. As the idiom went: hope springs eternal in lonely hearts.

"No problem. Do you mind if I sit with you while you wait for it to charge? Seems like there's all sorts of things we could talk about while you wait."

"Like what?" I raised an eyebrow, trying not to let

suspicion sharpen my tongue too much. Low profile, Ibby. Low profile.

He shrugged and moved towards the seat across from me. "I mean, you like coffee, I like coffee. You have a phone, I have a phone. Great place to start, right?"

I just stared, irritated. He put his coffee down on the table.

"Look." My tone was flat. "I'm not trying to be rude, but I would just like some time to myself."

He reddened and picked up his coffee again. "Sorry, just trying to make conversation." His dogged determination become a whine. "Let me get you a fresh cup as an apology. Please, it is the least I can do." He was actually reaching towards my cup, when someone placed a hand on his shoulder.

"You don't have to do that," came a warm, buttery voice. "But you do need to move on."

The persistent coffee drinker turned around, and though I couldn't see his face, his entire body seemed to deflate. Without looking back at me, he slumped away with a dull, "Sorry."

Grinning like a skull, Dillon Sark stood in a leather jacket, leaning into one hip, hands tucked into his jeans pockets. One look at his sly expression confirmed every suspicion I'd ever had … well, perhaps not 'every' suspicion. Jackie has dated some real pieces of work.

My lips pulled back from my teeth, and something primal and furious rose in my chest. The rings answered my unspoken call. Several metal items — spoons, picture frames, metal caps on the sugar and creamer dispensers — shifted a little in Dillon's direction. The handsome scoundrel never stopped smiling but caution flickered as his eyes widened.

Good, I thought with unabashed viciousness. I wanted him to know how easy it would be to blast him with metal.

"I know we are meeting for the first time, but I feel like we are past all of this, Ibukun." He gave a suave, casual sweep at the waiting metal projectiles. "Jackie's told me 'so much' about you. She'd be so happy we bumped into each other. Don't you think?"

He fished a phone from inside his jacket, turned his back to me, held it up and snapped a selfie that put me sitting over his shoulder. I was glaring, and he was grinning.

It took significant focus to keep a spoon from scooping out his right eye.

"She'll love it," he said, chuckling, dropping his phone back into the pocket. Shucking his coat, he tossed it into the corner of the booth. "The two people she loves the most in one place."

"What do you want?" I growled.

"May I sit?"

"No."

He slid across from me with liquid ease, then reclined with one hand resting on the table.

"Ibby, I don't know what idea you've gotten about me," he began, shaking his head slowly as his sculpted shoulders shrugged beneath a thin, white shirt. "I understand you are protective of Jackie, but your reaction seems a little … possessive. I know you called me here to tell me to stay away from your friend, but I'm hoping to convince you there is no need to see this as a competition."

I stared at him incredulously, knowing he was playing a game but not seeing the board.

"I never called you. You found me, and if you think I'm going quietly, you're dumber than the brutes you sent to my flat."

The mention of the flat tested his easy grin. He spoke in a low, controlled voice, the dazzling smile turning forced.

"Who called who are details that won't matter when I'm talking to Jackie next. What will matter is whether or not we've started collaborating." He leaned forwards, warming to his narrative. "Think of how happy you will make her if you've seen the error of your ways and help me. We'll take a night off just to celebrate, and with Jackie and I, you know we'll have a good time. If you thought she was wild before, just wait till I get that girl out. It'll be legendary." His expression slid into a lecherous, intimidating leer.

I wasn't sure what I wanted to do more: vomit or send a picture frame through his perfect teeth.

"If we haven't managed to put the past behind us and work together, she'll be so sad to learn of all the hateful things you said about us before fleeing London in a cloud of scandal. It will break her heart," he said with puppy dog eyes, before perking up. "But, I'll be there with big, strong shoulders for her to cry on."

He was like watching a *commedia dell'arte*, every expression mesmerisingly exaggerated. I realised I'd been spending so much time hatefully watching him, I hadn't been paying attention to my surroundings. I dared a look across the shop and spotted three familiar faces scowling at me through the front window. They didn't move to come in, and there was no way out of the front of the shop without passing them.

"Don't worry about them." Dillon waved cheerfully at the trio. "They're only here in the unlikely event that I'm not able to win you over."

My lip curled in a snarl. "I'm not feeling incredibly

convinced, Mr Sark. Perhaps you're suffering some performance anxiety."

Some honest emotion flickered across his face, an ugly spiteful thing. The hand on the table curled into a claw, and he opened his mouth to respond when a barista called his name.

"Be right back," he said, hissing the words with a death's-head grin.

Momentarily free from his scrutiny, I swept the room for another avenue of escape. I thought it utter arrogance on his part to assume he could just leave me sitting here while he fetched a coffee, but looking around, I understood.

The only other way out of the shop was a door beside the front counter. Dillon hadn't left me unattended so much as blocked the other exit while picking up his drink. It would be difficult to shoulder my way through to that door in a hurry. Plus, it could lead to a dead end, a pantry or storage room.

Working with him was out of the question, but I was beginning to think getting out of here quietly was not possible either. If I was to escape, it was going to be loud.

I stretched out mentally, feeling the fixtures, espresso machines, utensils and even the nails in the framing. So many options. But what actually gave me the chance to get out of here without getting killed, captured or hurting anyone else, excluding Dillon and his crew?

The germ of a plan formed as I sensed something on the floor, right in the shadow of the shop counter. I'd just started mentally tugging when Dillon slid into the booth.

"Now where were we? Oh yes, performance." He took a sip, his dark eyes glinting dangerously. "Sorry, I'm not living up to your expectations. Maybe I need to make things as clear as possible."

I plastered a neutral look on my face as my mind prepared things. Sweat sprang out on my forehead, but I was glad he was feeling chatty. The more time he spent talking, the more time I had.

"Now that we have found you, we're not going to lose you a second time. We know you were investigating Lowe at the Hall of Records, so we began to pick at that old scab again. Thanks for the lead. We're looking at it all with new eyes. If there is anything more to find, we'll find it."

I gave him a saccharine smile. "Jackie picks the low hanging fruit yet again."

His smile became a grimace of bared teeth, and his eyes stopped twinkling and started burning. I could feel his desire to reach across the table and strangle me. It was chilling to think this wolf in expensive clothing prowling around my best friend.

He growled, his fingers digging at the tabletop. "Working with us is preferable to not, because — as Lowe learned — not working with us leads to people vanishing. I'm sure you understand." He cocked a fine brow. "We are just being thorough."

And there it was. What he wanted, and what would happen if he didn't get it. I didn't let the cold rage show. "Your sales pitch could use some work, Sark," I said. "I'm not sure I can take a boy-band reject seriously."

"You little bi — " He never got to finish as a pastry fork flew into his groin, stopping short of penetrating his jeans. His eyes widened and darted to his lap as he jumped, then focused back up at me. He started to get up but stopped when I wagged a finger at him.

"I wouldn't do that if I were you," I warned and shifted back in the booth. "You see, I've spent the last few days practising. Honing my skills, one might say. It's amazing what I can do with metal."

I mentally nudged the fork and got an appreciable wince in return. Sweat began to bead on his smooth brow, and he became very still.

"Metal is such a beautiful thing. Much more pliable and willing to change than people realise. I can make all manner of things." I smiled at him. "That fork for instance. The handle is now a compressed steel spring, shaped with a catch. Any quick movements, and you'll be singing with the ladies for the rest of your days."

Dillon's face paled. His lips drew into a tight, ugly line. His gaze darted to the window, but he didn't signal his cronies.

"I'm going to go now." I got to my feet when I spied his coat. "It's a touch chilly, so I'm sure, as Jackie's mon chou, you won't mind it I take this."

He gave a thin hiss as I snatched up the coat, feeling his phone in the interior breast pocket. I put my own phone and charging cable into my bag.

"Best part about it? I don't even have to be here for it to stay in place." I threw on his jacket and looked down. "This fits surprisingly well. Those shoulders aren't as big and strong as you thought."

Dillon continued to seethe, and I felt him shift against the fork. With a mental flex, the fork tines scooted forwards. Dillon squirmed backwards. I kept the fork digging at him the whole way. He gasped.

"Don't test me, Mr Sark." I hooked a thumb towards the door. "Unless one of your lads is a medic."

The brutes outside had their noses plastered to the glass. I waved and blew a kiss to the hulking one who'd smashed me against the wall.

"I'm just a mouthpiece, you stupid bint," Dillon said, growling the words. "I'm a messenger. The message is:

partnership or execution. Walk away now, and you know which one you're signing. Hurting me won't change the outcome."

I winked, hoping I looked unaffected by his threat. "But it'll make me feel better."

He snarled some decidedly ungentlemanly things. More than one coffee house patron looked over in alarm, but I was done. The board was set. Though I couldn't see all the pieces, I now knew what the game was. I reminded myself I held an enemy hostage by his testicles, so these enemies, at least, were only men. Wicked, vicious men, but still just human beings.

And I, for better or worse, was more than that now.

I stood over by the shop counter halfway between the booths and the front window. Dillon's thugs were inching closer to the door, but their wide frames still filled the shopfront. I waved at them, and then held up a finger, mouthing the words, "One second."

All three paused, confused, and watched as I fished out the last of my cash and placed it on the counter.

"What would you like?" asked a barista with long, straight hair as she eyed the crumpled bills.

"An exit," I answered. "But I don't think this will cover it. It's all I have. Sorry."

"What?"

I unleashed my powers into the plan, hurling slivers of willpower in several directions. The edges of my vision blurred as the effort of it nearly knocked me out. I'd never tried to manipulate so much at once. Clinging to consciousness with mental fingernails, I watched my handiwork through bright flickering holes.

A trio of metal serving trays flew off the countertop, where I'd aligned them for the purpose. They struck the window, sending an explosion of shattered glass raining down on the three thugs. An instant later, each of them was broadsided by the trays. As those missiles were mid-flight, I yanked on the espresso machine — hard. It came free with a rip and a hiss, and I held it in mid-air for a moment, though the effort made my head throb.

Pulling the hissing, bubbling machine like a pet on a leash, I moved towards the door. Patrons screamed and scrambled out of the way. The brutes at the shattered window were slow at getting up, but by the time I'd forged a path to the door, the big one with the jutting jaw had risen. One bandaged hand made to bring a large, black pistol to bear. I hurled the espresso machine at him.

It hit him square in the chest as it spun end over end. Sprays of steam and gouts of boiling water erupted in every direction. The men on either side of the poleaxed companion screamed and pawed at their blistering skin. The big one hit the pavement like a sack of wet cement, and he didn't stir even as his face was blasted with scalding liquid.

The cost of the effort hit me.

My vision blacked out for a second. Thankfully, my fingers had already wrapped around the door handle, and muscular reflexes took over. I staggered drunkenly out the door, arms spinning to keep me upright. Righting myself as my vision returned, I threw a look over my shoulder before pelting down the street. None of the thugs pursued or shot at me. Dillon rushed to the front of the cafe, screaming curses.

I had exaggerated about the fork. It would have taken skill I didn't yet have, but Dillon didn't know that. Once I'd left the shop, I could no longer hold the fork against his groin. He discovered my ruse. The realisation on his face was the last thing I saw before I ducked down an alley.

I'd bought some time, but only enough to get to the university ahead of them. I hoped my knowledge of the place and Lowe's guidance would make the difference. I needed to get to the other set of rings before they did.

Chapter Sixteen

The campus was walled and gated, but a little work with some drain pipes, and I was up and over without anyone the wiser.

I didn't know if the porters had instructions to stop me if I tried to come on campus, but being detained by police would be a poor use of my time. I'd gotten ahead of Dillon's crew, but if they knew about Lowe and his connection to the rings, they'd have a good idea where I was heading. With my knowledge of the campus and my powers, I could navigate more easily, but they outnumbered me four to one.

I knew how to find the rings, so I had to capitalise on that while the knowledge was still exclusively mine.

I slid along the green before the lecture hall, shuffling past a few students with noses in their phones. Which reminded me I had Dillon's phone. I drew it out of the jacket. Other than smelling of cologne, I was growing to like the coat. It fit fairly well even if the arms were a little long.

The phone had a PIN, and after two careless attempts,

the device informed me I had two more tries before it reset. The phone was a dead end for now, but I slid it back into the pocket. It might be useful down the road if I ever managed to get access.

A soft drizzle misted down — hardly worth calling rain in London — as I followed a cobbled footpath to the courtyard before Brexlon Hall.

The hall had served as Lowe's home base, but since then had gone through several renovations. It had been converted to a residential hall, then to administration offices and now it was going through another repurposing. Scaffolding and plastic sheeting overlay the old stone building like peeling, flapping skin, glistening in the misty air. The venerable building — with its broad, squat frame and a vaguely pointed gable — resembled an old toad shedding its skin.

I searched the gardens and the shadows between the scaffolds. No signs of a living soul. I crept around the edge of the courtyard.

"Find the hidden attic access in the third floor men's lavatory, then look for a brick chimney column near the front of the building," I whispered. "Third brick, fifth row down from the top of the column, behind which is the key to free the lockbox hanging inside the flue."

"Actually, it's the fifth brick on the third row," a voice said at my shoulder.

Whirling around, hands balled into fists, my jaw dropped as I saw Lowe standing there, eyes wide.

"Terribly sorry for surprising you like that, my dear," he said, hands raised. He stood just clear of the shadows on the hem of the courtyard and wasn't even trying to talk quietly.

"Get out of sight and keep quiet," I said, hissing as I

slid deeper into the shadows, my gaze darting around the courtyard and across the face of Brexlon Hall.

"Ibby," he began with a display of tried patience. "I'm a ghost. The only person in danger of being detected is you."

"I thought you said you couldn't come with me," I growled, resuming my advance towards the hall.

"Failure of clarity on my part," he said, clearing his throat. The loud way he was speaking grated on my nerves. "I couldn't go with you on the train or on your various errands. I can only manifest at the museum, the university or the station. Anywhere else is impossible."

I tried to imagine a hundred years without real human contact, trapped in three locations you'd already spent most of your life around. That frightful thought cooled my irritation.

Unable to hold my dread fascination at bay, I asked, "Is it like walking into an invisible wall or something?"

Lowe shook his head as he strode along beside me, for all the world looking like any other professor chatting with a pupil as they moved between classes.

"Nothing so dramatic. If it had been, it might have saved me a good deal of confusion and frustrated experimentation over the first few years. Ah, I'd recommend you take the window there, behind that scaffold."

The window was on the north end of the hall where a section of the plastic sheeting had been cut back and the waist-height section of scaffold sat a metre out from the brick. It looked as though they were in the process of removing the old window, frame and all.

Slinking to the edge of the courtyard shadow, I then dashed behind the scaffolding. I hunkered down between the metal rods and the window frame, assessing my entrance. Lowe unceremoniously reached over and pushed on the panes. The window swung open.

"This is the only one with hinges that don't squeal terribly," he explained.

"Thanks," I said, breathily and began the delicate process of hauling myself through the window quietly. It wasn't easy. The bottom of the sill was level with my eye.

I liked to think of myself as being in moderately good shape. In secondary school, I ran regularly and took kick-boxing classes at a local community centre. While working an internship, I didn't have the time and energy for such things. I managed to get up there, carrying my bag along, but I sank down to the floor inside the building, a fresh sheen of sweat on my brow and my breath coming in gasps.

Lowe materialised next to me and walked down the hallway towards a pair of peaked doubled doors. He stepped on the threshold and was gone, as though he'd been edited out of existence. I shivered, the sweat on my body turning clammy.

Partnering with a ghost took some getting used to.

I climbed to my feet, looking up and down the corridor, when Lowe reappeared with a grave expression.

"The main foyer and the stairs are clear, but there may be someone upstairs already. I'm certain I heard footsteps."

My skin prickled up in goose flesh. I'd counted on being the first one on scene, and now that I wasn't, doubt hooked at my thoughts. What if this was an ambush? What if they were just waiting for me to get the rings for them?

"I'm not sure I can do this," I whispered, the utter confidence I'd had in the coffee shop feeling far away.

Lowe nodded but gave me an encouraging smile. "You've handled everything they've thrown at you so far, and quite handily, I might add."

"This is different." I didn't hide the panicked rush in my voice. "Every other time, it was them coming at me, not the other way around. I was just doing what I could to get away. I'm not a soldier or guardian or whatever these rings are supposed to make me."

In a fit of terror, I tugged at the rings, my fear momentarily overwhelming whatever grip they had on me. I nearly had them off when Lowe's hands closed around mine. His hands were cold, firm, but not unkind.

"Ibby, look at me," he commanded. His gaze met mine, and I couldn't look away. Will, pride, care, anger and sadness flickered in his eyes, now as pale as his hair in the reflected evening lights. Everything a professor, a teacher could feel at seeing a student giving up were in those eyes. As he looked at me and I at him, the geometries of emotion crystallised into one final shape: determination.

"Lowe, please." What I saw in his eyes woke a different fear. I didn't want to hear what he would say. What if I couldn't live up to it?

"Ibby, these rings." He opened his hands so I could see them. "They did not make you into anything. Everything was already there. The first time I saw you, I knew who you were. You are strength and will, bending but never breaking, and you are what this world desperately needs."

He released me, and I looked down at my hands, the rings glinting in the darkness.

"You've known you were capable of more, Ibby. It just scares you how much more."

I was scared, deathly so, but I chose to believe what he was saying. Dillon's threats echoed in my mind, his sneer materialising in my mind's eye. Now was the time to be strong. Strong like when I fought for my spot in my programme. Strong like when my parents died. Strong like when I chose to forge ahead for Uncle Iry's sake. I was strong then, and I could be strong now. Hopefully, I wouldn't break.

My ringed fingers tightened into a fist. My senses stretched out, feeling every scrap of metal down to the thumbtacks on a hallway bulletin board. Thinking they might come in handy, I put a hand out. The tacks came zipping over to my cupped palm.

"I might need you to provide a distraction," I remarked, my tone grim.

I met Lowe's eyes again, and he gave me a small, admiring nod. "At your service."

WITH LOWE ACTING as spectral reconnaissance, it was relatively easy to reach the third floor without alerting the intruders.

They were on the second floor, Lowe reported, and they were busy tearing apart the common, which had served as a conference room in Lowe's day. They'd already ripped into nearly all the offices on that floor, including — Lowe reported with irritation — his old office.

"Though, given the current decor," he mused, "I must say it's an improvement."

Creeping up the stairs and wincing every time one of the ransackers smashed something, I gave up talking to Lowe. When something gave a loud crash, I clenched my hand and then bit back a hiss of pain as the thumbtacks poked me. They'd seemed like a handy thing to have, all these tiny slivers of metal, given that I had no other weapons, but transporting a handful of pinpoints was tricky.

"I wonder if those ruffians have any idea how expensive that buffet was?" Lowe complained. "Not to mention the history it bore witness to!"

Lowe's commentary actually calmed my nerves, as I climbed onto the landing of the third floor.

"Not the Duchess's mirror!" Lowe groaned a second before the thud and the sound of splintering glass rose from beneath. "If only they'd drop dead, I could pummel them here and now," he grumbled, smashing a slender fist into his other palm. "Slack-jawed, inbred, tosspots ..."

The ghost's tirade continued as I stole down the hall towards the sign for the men's loo. It was dark in the lavatory. A few small frosted windows let in smudges of bleary illumination.

With my phone's light, I found the third stall and stepped inside. Pointing the phone's glow upwards, I could just see the faint outline of a square, which was set into the ceiling, the size of a trapdoor. I felt each screw anchoring the paint-lacquered panel in place.

Sliding the phone into the front of my new jacket, I adjusted it so the light just cleared the top of the pocket. Reaching a hand towards the screws, I mentally worked them loose, grinding my teeth as I spun them millimetre by bloody millimetre.

I wondered how much longer before the men downstairs moved to the third level or were joined by Dillon and his cronies. Every second could make the difference between a clean escape and having to fight. This thought gave impetus to my work. I could sense a metal ladder, folded and laying on top of the trapdoor.

I gave both the screws and the ladder a mental tug together, and the panel popped free. With a shriek from the rusted hinges, the ladder succumbed. I ducked as the panel dropped, but I was clipped by the descending ladder anyway, which felt as though someone had been keeping it greased all this time. Knocking the stall door open with a bang, I landed hard on my back. Breath whooshed from my lungs, and the thumbtacks sprayed across the floor.

I lay on the tiles, barely breathing and listening for a sign I'd been heard.

Lowe appeared, standing over me. "You really must be more careful."

I scowled but took his outstretched hand.

"You should hurry," he added as I mounted the ladder. "One of them received a call on his cellular device, and when he was done, the men redoubled their efforts. Someone may be coming this way very soon."

I didn't need further prompting. Without a backwards glance, I clambered up and drew out the phone light. The attic smelled of mould and dust and years of stillness. It was mostly bare except for a small pile of construction materials, shortboards and sections of rolled insulation. It took me a second to make out the stack of mortared bricks at the edge of the light's reach.

Bent almost double, I crept across the shallow space when I heard a rumble of voices beneath my feet.

They'd moved to the third floor.

Every step was a gamble. A squeaky board or groaning timber would betray me. Arriving at the chimney, I counted the bricks. The fifth brick on the third row came loose with a spatter of mortar crumbs, and then I had the key. A thin patina of orange corrosion covered its face, but I could feel the strength of the doughty metal.

Shuffling around the chimney, I found the blackened iron flue. The old metal here was more corroded, and I had to use my power to draw back the slide-bolt. It moved back with a scrape, and the door opened with a sharp squeak. I gave an involuntary gasp, my heart thrumming in my ears.

Lowe was squatting next to me. "They've started at the other end of the hall. Let's be quick, shall we?"

I nodded, pulling my heart out of my throat, and reached inside the flue, feeling along the upper lip of the access panel. A chain dangled there, and with some groping, the padlock and then the rectangular box came into my hands.

With only a little sticking in the padlock mechanism, the lock came free from one end of the chain. The other portion of the chain, still looped around the lock, was pulled down the flue, and the whole thing began to slither free. If I'd had more sense, I might've drawn the chain back up telepathically, but I was fixed on keeping the box in my other hand from falling. As such the chain, lock and key tumbled down into the dark. A distant clunk and rattle echoed from far below. I froze, holding my breath.

The ring's container was a little smaller than a shoe box, only thinner and made of polished wood. Once I blew the dust off, it shone a russet red, glossy in the light of the phone's torch. Its face was a series of laminated tiles making a vaguely floral design. They were arranged in a haphazard way with a few open spaces between: a puzzle box made in an old East Asian style.

"A gift from a friend in the Japanese antiquities department," Lowe explained at my shoulder.

I didn't jump this time. I was getting used to having the old wraith around.

I shook the box and heard a rattle.

"How do we open it?" I whispered, my eyes already crossing at the complexity of the pattern.

"Oh, bother," Lowe grumbled, his face knotting up in a grimace of frustration.

"You do remember, right?"

Lowe's face remained locked in that expression until—

similar to an image catching during a buffering stream — his whole body froze, flickered and flashed through snapshots of expression. I inched away from the shuddering ghost, clutching the box to my chest.

"Lowe?"

"I-I'm s-sorry," Lowe stammered, his speech catching like the first conversation we had. "I c-c-can't."

Then he was gone. No fading image. No puff of smoke, not even a last lingering word. He was just gone.

"Lowe," I whispered tentatively, but I knew he wouldn't respond. Something about his sudden departure seemed serious, if not absolute. For the time being, I was on my own.

I strained to hear the men downstairs. I could have laughed at the absurdity of my situation. Hiding in an attic and wishing a ghost would come back to help me escape the living, rather than the other way around.

The sound of the ransackers was a distant commotion, barely audible. That gave me the confidence to move towards the hatch that opened to the lavatory. Once I'd escaped, I could figure out how to open the puzzle box. If all else failed, I'd just smash the thing open, though it would be a shame to destroy something so pretty.

I lifted the box and rattled the rings, sensing every contour and the potent hum of their unique composition.

I made to put the box in my bag and discovered it wouldn't fit. I looked at my school books. They were expensive and weighted with knowledge I needed to pass classes and grow as an archaeologist. I'd been carrying them everywhere with me.

With some sorrow, I traded the books for the ring box. Returning to the ladder, I began my descent. Halfway down came the sounds of sighing and the trickle of liquid into a basin. I froze, realising what I was hearing, and hung there suspended halfway between the ceiling and the stall, my heart galloping in my chest.

My pulse doubled as I realised I hadn't turned off my phone light. It was a miracle he hadn't noticed it reflecting off the back walls. One handed, I tried to draw the phone out of the jacket pocket. The ladder gave a little squeak.

The trickling sound stopped.

I didn't dare turn around and bathe the lavatory in the white light of my phone. Every muscle tense, I hardly breathed. Every sound seemed amplified including my hammering heart.

There was a grunt followed by a zip, the shuffling of clothing and I found a thin slice of hope. Maybe I hadn't cut him off midstream. Maybe his business was finished.

Heavy steps moved behind me, heading towards the door. He passed the sinks without stopping. I was so close to a clean escape. Then came a curious mutter and the scuff of shuffling feet. An eternal second of surprised silence, and then an angry shout.

"What the bloody hell!"

I flew down the last rungs of the ladder and shot out of the stall, just as he came around. He gave a snarl as the light from my jacket pocket caught his unprepared eyes.

He was dressed in a construction worker's neon yellow vest, complete with a white hard hat and sleeves rolled up to the elbows. His pants were coated with powdered drywall, and slivers of wood clung to his sleeves. One gloved hand held a crowbar, while the other shielded his face from my light.

He started to holler again when I spotted the thumbtacks where they'd fallen on the floor. With a sweep of my arm I sent them zipping like a cloud of hornets. They flew at his face and upraised hand, biting into fabric and flesh.

He shrieked and swung his crowbar. I had to dive off

my feet to keep from being brained. He tripped over my legs and fell, smashing into the stall door hard enough to crack the wood.

On all fours, I scrambled to get clear. Remembering what was in his hand, I gave the metal a hard shove. Flexing as though it were made out of rubber, the crowbar took the momentum of his swing and whipped around hard. The sudden wrenching force twisted his wrist. There was a cracking sound, and he released the crowbar with a whimper.

I was on my feet and out the door as he lay on the floor, curling his whole body around his wrist.

Five steps down the hall, three more burly ransackers blocked my way. I skidded to a halt on the polished floor. Mean eyes and hard faces in the glare of my phone eyed me with a mix of anger and interest. I must've looked like easy pickings. Their faces split into predatory grins. One with a crowbar in his hand shared a knowing look with his compatriot hefting a claw hammer. The third one, short but with arms like tree trunks and a barrel of a body, raised two-handed a sledge as though it were a broom handle.

"Come 'ere, lass," the sledge-wielder rumbled with a gap-toothed, yellow smile. "Come an' I'll give yeh a kiss."

Though none of them were slight, they couldn't block the whole hallway. I faked a step left before lunging right.

No dice.

All three of them ignored my feinted step and sprang in front of me, weapons ready. I tried to adjust course, zipping back the way I came, but I was too close. The sledger bulled towards me on stumpy legs, checking me hard with the wooden haft of his impromptu weapon. Breath exploded from my lungs as I flew backwards, landing on my rump, then rolling over in an awkward flop.

My phone fell out of my pocket, and the light went off when it struck the floor. The hallway descended into broken twilight. My bag gaped, spilling the puzzle box onto the floor. The trio advanced, their eyes gleaming greedily like subterranean misers. My lungs felt as though they were collapsing as I tried to suck in air.

"What's that you got there, girly?" one cooed, as they leaned forwards eagerly.

"What might be in that pretty package, I wonder," another tittered in an unctuously high-pitched voice.

"Looks like the little witch just made our jobs a lot easier," grated the rough throated voice of the sledge-wielder.

Air began to fill my lungs again. Anger and desperation pushed me to my knees. As I shoved upwards, the rings on my hand rasped against the floor, reminding me of their presence. Reminding me that I was going about this all wrong. I was so scared, so desperate to get away, I was going about this like the old Ibby. I clenched my ringed hand into a fist. I needed to stop trying to run like Ibby, and start fighting my way out like … an Inconquo.

I put one unsteady leg under me and — with a grunt — forced myself to stand.

Alerted to a change, the ransackers looked up from the box, their faces masked in the half-light, but the ugly humour was gone. They sensed something different, and they didn't like it. No jokes or taunts this time, they advanced, weapons raised. Too bad they didn't realise their implements of iron and steel were under new management.

The one with the claw hammer came first, swinging the weapon with an aim to bury it in my skull. I could feel the metal of the head running down all the way into the plastic grip. With an angry jab, I sent the metal head sliding through its grip until it split the plastic. The misshapen hammer fell from its maker's hand as shards of broken handle bit into his palm. I sent a sharp kick into the side of his leg as he barrelled blindly past me. His weight folded around his wrenched knee, and he fell with a scream.

The others came at me, eyes wide.

The sledge swung in a wide arc, determined to either force me back or put me in an awkward position for the long-handled crowbar to make a strike. Yanking on the upraised crowbar, I brought it down on the back of the sledger's head. An off-handed mental shove forced the sledge to swing wide as its wielder ploughed into the ground, senseless. The hard hat he wore had saved his life, but he and his huge maul were out of the fight for good.

The last one stared, stunned into a wide-mouthed gape. His bemusement became terror as I reached out and forced the long-handled crowbar to twist in his hand like a living thing. He screeched and tried to throw it down, but I wound it around the front of his body like a snake, pinching his arms to his chest.

I stalked forwards as he squirmed and danced, trying to work his arms free. Scooping up my bag, I slid the ring box inside. He never saw the step kick that took him hard across his posterior and sent him tumbling to the floor. I didn't bother to look his way as I went for the stairs, though I could hear him panting and wheezing.

As a bonus, I found my phone on the way there, and I slid it into the coat next to Dillon's phone.

I walked down the stairs, head high but ears and eyes open. The halls were empty and quiet, minus the distant shuffling movements and groans from above.

I'd done it again.

The realisation was incredible, almost intoxicating. Is this what was meant by the thrill of victory? This wasn't a thrill; this was a high. Despite the ache in my ribs and some scuffed shins, I felt damn near invincible. Three times now, bad men had come at me, and three times I'd beaten them all. I wasn't just a mystic guardian: I was a bloody superhero!

I felt the metal fittings on the main entrance hall doors and the scaffolding in front of it. Throwing both my hands out to punctuate the mental blast, the huge oak doors swung wide, the scaffolding dancing out in front of them. Plastic sheeting flapped and fluttered as I strode out of Brexlon Hall, victorious.

Chapter Seventeen

That buoyant exultation carried me all the way to the edge of campus, where I used my drainpipe trick to handily waltz over the wall and into the alley.

You know that thing they say about pride?

Sharp snaps whip-cracked through the air, and the bricks behind me puffed up in a spray of burst mortar and brick shards. A few shards hit my face, and I screamed as the shrapnel cut a gash over my eye. I felt hot blood trickle down the side of my face.

Bullets whizzed by and buried themselves in the wall, where they throbbed dully.

A blow cracked across my ear. My head rebounded off the wall, and the world became a riot of strobing colours and watery sounds. I slumped down onto one knee, and another impact broke across my shoulder blade. I sank onto hands and knees as blood dripped freely from my head. Black haze crowded my vision and pain swelled, blocking out rational thought.

A voice carved its way through the fuzzy moshpit of

my senses. It was a cruel, ranting gasp of sound as more impacts came.

"… think you can get away with this you stupid …"

Blows drove against my side, crashed into my stomach and ribs, and bounced my body off the brick. Curiously, the pain was going numb. I should be hurting more, but all I felt was the dull rocking force of the beating and the rebounds in my nerveless body.

"… smirk at me now you, ugly, little …"

A shrinking voice inside my battered head told me the numbness was a bad sign, but the thought was drowned out by the mad voice.

"… I'll cut those rings off your filthy corpse, you …"

The world was grey and indistinct. Something deep inside me fought and clawed, willing me not to surrender to the inviting oblivion. My vision came into focus for a moment, and there was a flash of his face. Dillon, his expression twisted into a horrible mockery of his normal features. Bulging eyes and gnashing teeth lurked beneath hair gone stringy with sweat.

A sudden stark spotlight highlighted every grotesque crease and cranny. The light intensified, washing out his features, and the muddled sounds merged into a rattling roar. Dillon's terrible gaze swept towards the brilliant light, and I watched in confusion as his countenance shifted into fear. The roaring noise was incredible now.

Dillon flew away as the light blinded me, then roared past in a flash of metal and petrol fumes. I tried to get up using the wall for support, but my body didn't want to obey. My knees trembled uncontrollably. Only one eye seemed to have vision.

The alley was in chaos. A growling motorcycle slewed around, chasing Dillon, while a brute with patches of blistered skin across his face and hands fired wild shots at the biker. Dillon sprinted down the alley, arms pumping and my bag dangling from one fist. I felt a blunt sort of anger and desire to retrieve the bag, but my body was gradually awakening to its injuries, and those were quickly eclipsing everything else. My hand rose to my head as I tried to collect my thoughts. Everything felt sticky inside and outside my skull. A wave of nausea ploughed over me, and I curled around my aching stomach before vomiting onto the dirty cobblestones. Gagging and retching, the stabbing pains in my side brought back focus with razor-sharp clarity. Even the eye that had been out of commission regained some sight.

Dillon rounded the corner at the far end of the alley. My bag, still bouncing along on its strap, disappeared with him. The motorbike slowed to a stop, and the black, insectile helmet gazed after Dillon, before swinging back my way. The rider appeared torn between following Dillon or racing back the way she'd come.

Yes, she. Men were not built like that, though I knew quite a few lucky women who might match.

She came to her decision when the gun thug, who had been reloading, started firing again. Bullets, hastily blasted down the alley, zipped past her. She revved her engine and shot out the mouth of the alley.

The brute — the big one I'd hit with the espresso machine — stomped after the biker, firing off another useless shot before stopping. I watched him, fighting for each pain-laced breath, as he turned to glare at me. I saw the stained bandage on his hand, the bubbled welts all over his skin, and the way he stood, as if his back had stopped bending properly. A fresh quiver of fear shook me. He lusted for vengeance.

Almost lazily, he walked towards me, pistol dangling from his big fist. He wanted me to know he was in control.

When he spoke, his thick voice was dripping with smug satisfaction.

"I could hurt you so badly," he declared. "But I think I'll just end you and finally take those rings off your hand. Hang Sark's orders."

The pistol rose, and the world moved like it was caught in syrup. My mind worked only marginally faster, but it would have to be enough. The handgun was, to my surprise, composed mostly of non-metals, but there were a few things, not least of all the bullets. The suppressor jutting from the pistol barrel was a tube of baffled metal, and I fixed my attention on this.

As badly beaten as I was, forcing the handgun down was like gripping something with a broken hand. I sobbed with the effort. Still, with his first trigger pull, the bullet struck the base of the wall a foot to my right.

He snarled and fought against me with his whole body, leaning against the gun with his considerable mass. I released my hold, letting him whiplash the other way, and his second shot went wide to my left.

The third shot would not miss. I didn't have the strength to wrestle with him, and we both knew it. He smiled at me then, and he took his time levelling the pistol at my face.

"Get stuffed, you mangy cow," he spat out the words and pulled the trigger.

I couldn't muster the mental effort to grapple with him over the handgun, but I had enough strength to wrinkle the metal in his suppressor, turning it into a long, metal stopper.

The firing pin struck the primer, igniting and detonating the powder. The bullet hurled forwards, carried on a tide of erupting chemistry. It met the pinched-off suppressor, and with nowhere to go, Newton's Third Law came into effect.

The pistol barrel and suppressor exploded. The ear-splitting pop paired with a sharp 'ping' as fragments shot off in all directions.

I threw my hands in front of my face, so I didn't see the immediate effects on the gunman's hand, but as I looked between my fingers a second later, I watched him reel through a thin cloud of smoke. The pistol had fallen from his bleeding hand, but it was little comfort as he came barrelling through the grey haze. His undamaged hand wrapped around my throat, and he dragged me up against the wall until my feet were off the ground. Dangling there in front of him, face to face, I got full view of his incredible, unflinching rage. He looked as though he was going to choke the life out of me if it was the last thing he did. I clawed feebly at his crushing grip.

Things were getting spotty. My vision became a tube, then a tunnel. But, there was a light at the end of it. Wavering, white and bright and … accompanied by a snarling engine. There was a jarring thud.

My executioner released my neck, and I collapsed like a marionette without a puppeteer. I crumpled to the cobblestones, hacking, fingers at my neck as my throat burned and screamed. My lungs wailed for air. Tears leaked from my eyes, blurring my vision. I scrubbed at my eyes with the sleeve of my jacket and looked up, still coughing.

The biker circled around and came to idle in front of me. She holstered a collapsible baton on her hip.

Knees wobbling, it felt as though I took years to get to my feet, but I managed to sag against the wall. Gazing at the woman on the bike, I managed to mouth, "thank you."

The biker threw up the visor of her helmet. Her eyes

were familiar, though in my brutalised state I couldn't place them. Dark and flashing dangerously, they took me in. She held out her hand, shouting over the engine's throaty purr, "Phone."

I stared stupidly, but when she reiterated the demand, I slowly complied. It seemed strange that she'd come back just to rob me of my phones, but I was past caring. I wanted to lapse into a coma peacefully, if it wasn't too much to ask.

I held out my phone as well as Dillon's. She took them and settled back onto her metal steed. With mechanical efficiency, she disassembled both devices, separating casing, battery and phone. She popped open a rear compartment and unceremoniously dumped the dismembered plunder inside. She snapped the compartment shut and faced me.

"Come on!" She held out a hand.

I stared into her eyes, those familiar, lovely spheres, and though I felt like lying down, I forced myself to reach out. She helped me onto the back of the bike where I wrapped my arms around her.

"Hang on tight," she called. With a hungry cry from the motorcycle, we tore off into the night.

MY RESCUER RACED up roads and down alleyways, interchanging between major thoroughfares and side streets, seemingly at random. Sometimes, we were hurtling along fast enough the wind stung my face, and at other times, we coasted, barely faster than a jog. I gave up on working out her destination, and after passing the same Indian restaurant for the third time, I realised she wanted to ensure no one was following us.

It was a comfort she didn't seem intent on dragging me

off to some evil lair posthaste, but the evasive tactics allowed me to replay the events. I groaned and set my forehead against her back.

I'd lost the other set of rings, failing at the one task I'd set out to accomplish.

A weight that had nothing to do with bodily fatigue settled over me until it was all I could do to hold on. I bit back tears as we coasted around another corner.

Failed. Utterly.

If it hadn't been for the mystery woman, I would have also lost the rings I was wearing and my own life to boot. I shivered, the realisation of how close I'd come to death, mere seconds, cast my confidence on leaving Brexlon Hall into a new light. I'd been so stupid, so arrogant, and in doing so, I'd lost everything or damn near close to it.

I could have screamed my anger and self-loathing to the skies. As it was, the fires of my anger sputtered out before we merged onto the next street, and I was left feeling a sickening emptiness.

What now?

Dillon had the second pair of rings, and they might be enough to set Kezsarak free. I still didn't know all the ways that would be bad, but if that demon's torment of my dreams was any evidence, the world could do without him running free. I shuddered at the thought, remembering the crushing gears and wishing for death.

No, if nothing else, for my own sanity, I needed to keep Kezsarak buried deep in whatever prison he was in.

But how?

I felt a shift in my ride's stance, and then we were gliding into a parking lot just off a busy street I didn't recognise. The expanse was nearly empty of cars, a bare, concrete square between a petrol station and a shuttered collections agency. A few streetlamps cast pools of light, but the rider piloted us to a patch of black shadow between them. We came to a stop, the rider throwing out her legs to brace the bike as it gave a final chuff, before she slid out the kickstand.

I'd never ridden a motorcycle before, so the etiquette of a dismounting passenger was lost on me. I peeled my arms from around her, my locked muscles protesting. She swung a leg over and kept a hand on the bike as I managed a clumsy dismount. My whole body throbbed, and the tense ride had done nothing to help.

Standing on the pavement sent knives of pain through my ribcage, stealing my breath. I doubled over, willing air into my tightening lungs.

"You look awful but there's still fight in you," the biker said, chuckling as she removed her helmet. "You nearly squeezed the life out of me."

A flash of dark hair flipped up, and I was staring at those familiar eyes again, set in a striking face I couldn't readily forget.

"Daria?" I wheezed at the woman from the university lavatory.

"Yes, love," she said, nodding. "Hello, again. I suppose you'd like an explanation."

"You think?" I had just enough breath to put force behind the words, but I made the mistake of trying to stand up to deliver them. A second later, I was wincing and gasping, one hand on my knees, the other bracing my side.

"Take it easy," she said, putting a hand on my back. "Sark laid into you pretty badly. You must have really hacked him off. We need to get you looked at."

A lorry barrelled by, laying on its horn. We both jumped at the sudden blast. When I looked at Daria, a cry of new shock escaped me.

Her dark eyes gleamed like those of a night-time

predator reflecting torchlight. Her lips peeled back to reveal needle-sharp teeth. In a flash, the monster was gone, and she was pretty Daria once more, but I was past believing it was a trick of the light.

"We need to go," she said, reaching out to help me straighten.

I lurched back and nearly folded in two at the pain arcing up through my body. Both my hands wrapped around my ribs, and I snarled. "Like hell. There is no we!"

Dary's face bowed with genuine hurt.

"Ibby, please," Daria pleaded. "You're hurt." But she took a step back.

Fear and anger gave me a strength I didn't think I could muster. With a grunt of effort, I shot my hand out and curled my fingers into a claw. The metal clasps of her biker boots stretched like elastics to the opposite foot and, with a snap, bound themselves together.

"Stay back," I said, panting as I sank down onto my knees. I wanted to melt into the pavement cracks, but I stoked the last embers of my desperate rage. I had to stay awake, had to stay on guard.

She looked down at her hobbled feet and sighed. "Ibby, this is childish. Why would I rescue you if I wanted to hurt you?"

Dary's eyes, so vulnerable in her young face, flashed with irritation as she looked up. She stared at me with a long exhale. I glimpsed for just a second the incredible mind working behind those eyes, and saw experience there. Her body and face said young woman, probably my age, but those eyes said she was frighteningly old.

"Who … are you?" I asked, finding it wasn't just breathing that was difficult. Forming my thoughts into specific words was getting harder too.

The woman crossed her arms and glared at me for a

second, and it was hard to keep my eyes from wandering to the collapsed baton on her hip. The aluminium alloy of its telescoping shaft was ready to betray its mistress at any sign from me. I took what comfort I could from that.

"I'm not a student, as I led you to believe. I was at the university on the lookout for signs of an organisation I've worked with in the past."

First Dillon, now her; didn't anybody at university just go to school?

I shook my head and settled into a cross-legged slump on the pavement. I needed to sit down before I fell over. My head felt heavy, but at least breathing seemed easier.

"What organisation?"

"They call themselves the Group of Winterthür."

I stared, unsure if it was just my injuries or my ignorance that left me clueless.

"They're the group that betrayed Lowe all those years ago and the one Sark is currently working for," Dary explained. "They have agents in academia so I was waiting for something to shake loose."

"You … you worked … for them?"

"With. Not for," Daria clarified. "I'm a freelancer, but things didn't go well last time, and I was looking to even the score. Sark is just one in a long line of miserable gits employed by them."

She called Dillon a miserable git. How hilarious and endearing. I giggled, not really knowing why I found it so funny. Something clicked in my side when I laughed.

Dary's expression became one of grim concern. "I'm on your side, Ibby."

She gestured towards her feet. "Ibby, I'm begging you, please. For your own sake, undo this and let me help you. Much longer, and I'm not sure if I can get you to help on time."

For a second, I wasn't sure what she was talking about, and that seemed funny too. Then the metal of her altered boots sang out to me, and I released the mental grip I'd forgotten I was maintaining. I felt like letting go of a lot of things right about then, not the least of which was my bladder.

"I really have to wee." I giggled again, then: "Ow."

With a sigh, Daria helped me slowly to my feet and braced me with an arm.

"Where is Lowe?" she asked as my head lolled back.

I stared up into the dark sky with the corona of the streetlight at the upper edge of my vision, a reverse sunrise.

"I'm cold," I muttered and gave a half-hearted shiver.

Dary's fingers squeezed my arm, and her breath felt warm on the side of my face. "Ibby, for the sake of your life, how do you get to Lowe?"

Lowe? Lowe was gone. Gone like I was going. It wouldn't matter if I told her.

"British Museum Station," I slurred, my tongue a stranger in my mouth. "Covent to ghost station."

The dark sky swelled, pressing on me as it thickened and roiled. For a second, I saw flashes of light, like lightning bugs, and I recognised the red-orange flashes as cinders. From a flurry of those, burning eyes materialised in the drooping sky. I tried to scream, but darkness swallowed me.

Chapter Eighteen

My existence had shrunk to two distinct points.

First was a single finger that extended out from the machine, which I could twitch and crook uselessly. It was a futile movement, but trapped as I was, I kept curling and uncurling, terrified that small movement would be gone too, and I would be entombed in the gears completely and eternally. That single finger was my only defiance.

Second, and even less pleasant, was the incredible burden of breathing. My chest clenched between the twisting teeth of spoked wheels. Every instant was a compressed eternity, where I was certain I couldn't force my tortured organs to draw in one more breath, and then somehow, painfully sucked in enough oxygen to stay alive. Never enough to stave off the panicked pressure of needing another breath, but just enough so I couldn't enjoy the oblivious darkness beyond the machine.

Thoughts, even terror and despair, wouldn't form into anything coherent as I tried to drag in another breath.

UNDERSTAND.

The voice was there, gloatingly patient, reverberating up through the gears so I could feel the spiteful satisfaction vibrating in my distended bones and crushed flesh.

KNOW.

If they were commands or declarations, or both, I didn't know, but either way, they hinted at a subtle shift in the voice. The rage was absent, and between breaths, I realised the machine was cold now, its furious heat quenched. My finger curled in and brushed the metal, cool to the touch.

YESSS.

The bitterness was still there, a vast ocean of malice filled with millennia of resentment, but the storm had passed for now. The voice rested, settling to the bottom of its hateful depths, content to watch me. The horror of this terrible nonexistence ate at my mind, gnawing with dreadful teeth. The voice wanted me to stay there, perhaps for a million eternities, to soak in its venomous sea as it watched me trapped in that cramped state of bare existence.

BEAUTIFUL.

A kind of awful contentment which had no place with that word suffused the machine as a low atonal hum. It came from a being, who understood time as an abstraction I couldn't hope to digest. My suffering would be absolute, inescapable and endless in a way that beggared my mind. My twitching finger and gasping breath were the only landmarks in a wasteland I would circle, over and over and over again. I had nothing else. I was nothing else.

FOREVER.

I WOKE up screaming and shivering.

Lurching upwards, hands tried to push me back down … into the machine. I wailed and fought them hard, clawed, squirmed, kicked and bit.

"Ibby, please," a man's voice came with the sound of breaking glass.

"Damn it, Lowe, just hold her!" A woman this time.

My mind lashed about at the same time as my body, reaching reflexively for metallics at hand. Finding delicate tines of metal as fine and strong as spider silk, I raked them around me with slashing fingers.

"Daria, look out!"

The tines struck something solid, and a woman's scream of pain drowned out my own. The hands released me, and I lurched to my feet. The world reeled wildly, and I swung out like I could grab a hold of it and force it to stop. As I swung, the metal tines twisted, and another scream rang high and loud.

"Ibby, that is enough!" the man bellowed.

Pain blasted sharply across my cheek.

My head whipped to the side, my neck cracked. One hand flew to the sting at my face. My cheek smarted, but the burning sensation, juxtaposed with the chilly touch of the hand, cleared the fog of madness and fear.

I wasn't in the machine. Theirs wasn't 'the voice.'

The world resolved into the commons of Museum Station. I was standing in front of the obelisk, trembling and sweating. Lowe glared, looking angry and ashamed. Behind him, Daria lay on the floor, clutching an arm where half a dozen syringes were buried.

"What's going on?" Slowly it was dawning. It was me who'd sent the needles flying into Daria. The fine spider's silk of metals.

Lowe relaxed a little, but his eyes shone with a fierce animation. "You were hurt." He swept a hand towards Daria. "She brought you here to recover."

I looked from Lowe to Dary, who glared up at me from her bleeding arm.

"You're bloody welcome!" Gingerly Daria touched a needle and gave a hiss of pain.

"I … I'm sorry," I croaked. "I thought you were …"

"You should lie down." Lowe nodded at the cot on the floor. Next to it was a pile of clothes, scattered medical supplies and a few broken bottles. I felt very cold and tired, but I didn't want to lie down, fearing a return to the hellish machine. I wrapped my arms around myself … and discovered I was nearly naked.

Soft linen swaddled me from the lowest rib to above my breasts. Other than the bandage and my underwear, I didn't have a stitch of clothing on. Cheeks burning, I dropped into the cot. Snatching up the rumpled sheet, I pulled it up to my chin.

Daria sat on the ground, still testing the crumpled syringes, finding them bent and unwilling to slide free easily. Lowe stood over her. His posture was that of a man dealing with something dangerous.

"Do you need anything?" he asked, though I noticed he was not doing anything which might bring him closer to her.

Daria left off tugging at the syringes and looked up at him, her expression saturated with that same spooky light from earlier. "I'll be fine, Lowe. Just smarts. Fetch me the kit?"

Lowe nodded and turned towards me. "Ibby, would you please pick up that knapsack under your cot?"

I found a very old but well-cared for bag of leather with a bronze-latched top and canvas straps. It hung open, medical paraphernalia a visible jumble inside.

I stood, still holding the sheet around me with one arm and an elbow, and shuffled forwards with the bag.

Lowe met me halfway and took the bag. I waddled back, careful of the broken glass that littered the floor. Spying a rumpled pile of clothes, I recognised them as my thrift store purchases. Even Dillon's jacket lay at the bottom of the pile. Snatching these up, I began to dress while stealing glances towards Lowe and Daria. Lowe had handed off the bag and resumed his stiff posture, while

Dary, after fishing out some tweezers and gauze, began the extraction.

The first syringe slowly slid free as Daria controlled her body and breathing with obvious effort. By the time several centimetres of needle had emerged, I was both impressed with her and mortified with myself. The events of my awakening were still fuzzy, but I remembered the dream. Every detail made me feel queasy and quivery. I knew why I was in such a state when I woke up, but it didn't make it any easier to see the results.

"Is there anything I can do to help?" I called as I stood to pull on my jeans.

"It doesn't need anything from us," Lowe answered and flapped a hand. "Just sit down and stay calm please."

My hackles rose at the dismissal, followed by a cold splash of contrition.

You lost the other set of rings. Some Inconquo.

I sank back down onto the cot and stared at the floor. Lowe's spirit had been waiting for me for a century, and I failed my first 'mission' spectacularly. I'd nearly died, had to be rescued, then nearly killed Daria too. I looked at the rings on my fingers and thought about stripping them off and leaving. Maybe I wasn't a true Inconquo after all. Lowe was mistaken.

Dary muttered something to Lowe. I looked up to see them staring at me. Daria's expression was concerned while Lowe's was stern as steel. Brows furrowed like grey thunderclouds, his mouth a grim line. I wasn't ready for the surge of shame and sorrow that welled up at the sight. Lips trembling, I wrapped my arms around myself.

"I'm sorry," I sobbed, the words sounding leaden. "I'm so sorry, Professor."

I wanted to hide my face, but I didn't, determined to bear his judgement, his scorn. I deserved it.

Lowe's scowl crumbled. "It's going to be fine." He shook his head slowly, bemused. "It isn't human, after all. Not anymore."

I blinked in confusion, my mouth hanging open. What was he talking about?

"Thank you, dear." Dary hissed as another syringe came free, and she applied some gauze. "You've managed to insult me and confuse Ibby, all in one fell swoop. Bravo!"

I pressed my hands to my temples and squeezed. My addled brains must have missed something vital.

"She's upset." Lowe turned back to Dary, exasperated. "She doesn't need to think she's hurt an actual person."

Daria looked up from her ministrations with a withering glare. "How sweet of you, James," she replied coldly. "If you prick me, do I not bleed?"

Lowe gave a dismissive shrug as a third syringe came free. "So do scorpions and spiders," he replied. "No one gets upset when 'they' get squashed."

Dary ceased pulling on a syringe and stabbed the tweezers towards him, eyes flashing that feral light. "Now listen here you pompous, self-righteous, arrogant —"

"What the hell is going on?" The question burst out of me like an explosion. My hands gripped the frame of the cot hard enough that my knuckles to stained the skin. "You're telling me she isn't a she, and she's not debating the issue? You're fighting like an old married couple." My voice trembled. "And why does no one seem to care I failed so badly at getting the rings?"

Lowe and Daria shared a knowing look. Dary went back to removing the needles while Lowe came to kneel in front of me. He held out a hand, and I took it. The familiar chill of his touch was a comfort I desperately needed.

"That you are alive and that we still have the other

rings is victory enough for today. Given what you were up against, things could have gone very badly."

I started to argue, but a gentle squeeze of my hand and a brisk shake of his head quieted me.

"No, Ibby, you need to hear me. This fight has been going on for ages. Literally. We need to take the long view. This is a battle that can't be won in one night or even a year. I was able to scrape a few successes in three decades of effort, and no one was shooting at me."

He wiped a few tears from my cheek and raised my chin when it began to sink.

"Don't be ashamed. That you are alive is proof of strength that few possess."

I met the eyes of the ghost and saw the sincerity, and more importantly, the trust in his eyes. He still believed in me.

"All right." My breath shook. I used my free hand to palm further tears away. "I'll trust your experience on this one."

"Wise decision." Lowe smiled, and with a final squeeze, he let go of my hand but did not rise. "If anything, I should be the one apologising. I abandoned you when you needed me in Brexlon Hall. I'm sorry, Ibby."

Lowe appeared deeply embarrassed, unable to look me in the eye.

"What happened?" I asked gently.

Lowe shrugged, crossing his arms. "To be honest, I can't recall much of what happened after we entered Brexlon Hall. The incident affected me in ways I don't understand."

I might have dropped the subject then, but Dary stood, wrapping her arm in linen.

She eyed Lowe with a softness that surprised me. "What happened at Brexlon Hall?"

I looked at her and then Lowe, uncertain of the nuances.

Lowe raised his gaze and gave me a sad nod. "It's fine, Ibby. It may be able to tell us something important."

Again with 'It,' and with the pronoun came the memories of Dary's shining eyes and serrated grin. I stared at Daria for a second and then thought I might be better off just telling my story to Lowe with her listening.

"One moment you were my wingman, then you went like a scratched record. Then you were just gone. You were really upset about them trashing the hall, but that wasn't when you disappeared. That happened once I had the puzzle box."

"Puzzle box?" Daria asked, her tone sharp and her brows pinched.

I nodded. "I asked you how to open it, and you said that you couldn't remember. That's when you started acting strange. Then you vanished."

"I'm sorry," Lowe said softly, but his eyes cut towards Daria with something like longing.

"Ibby, this puzzle box …" Dary inched towards me, her face knotted with wonder and suspicion. "Were its tiles a mix of shapes and flower patterns? And was the wood red in colour?"

I nodded a yes to both questions. She brightened with each affirmative.

"Don't make it into something it's not," Lowe said sharply.

A soft smile spread across Daria's face, coming on like a new dawn. "Oh, James," she cooed with glowing warmth. "I knew it meant something to you." She shot me a pleased look. "The box was a gift from me."

The ghostly professor looked mortified and straightened with his arms at his sides, eyes looking to the ceiling, the very picture of a man doing his utmost to endure. This lasted a few seconds before he heaved a great sigh.

"Now is not the time for … for this."

Curiosity strained my nerves. "What am I missing?"

Dary took a step towards Lowe, her movement that of a woman approaching a wounded animal. "James, perhaps you would like to retire to another part of the station while Ibby and I have a chat."

Lowe still would not look at her, but his voice was strained and beginning to slur again. "W-we need to ssstart plan-ning our nex-sst step."

Dary was close enough to touch him now, and one hand was upraised ready to rest on his shoulder. She never closed the distance.

"It is going to take time to track Sark so why don't you rest while I get Ibby comfortable. I'll fill her in on what she needs to know. Please, before you disappear again."

Lowe looked like he wanted to argue the point further, but the animus drained from his face and he gave a sad smile. "You always-s knew what was b-best."

He walked away, his figure blended with the shadows and shapes around him. Then he vanished.

Daria stared after Lowe, a tear rolling down her cheek, the age and fierceness of her gaze was gone. I could again believe she was a young woman trying to find her path in life, just like me.

Daria wiped away her tears, straightened and faced me. "Years before his death, James and I were in love. I'd been posing as an expert in Far Eastern studies when we met, and as our friendship became intimate, he shared his secret research with me about the Inconquo, a subject I am, unfortunately, well acquainted with."

She crossed to the cot and began to gather up the remaining medical supplies and put them into her kit.

"Before me, he was concerned only with the mystery of an ancient cult, but for his sake and that of his research, I pushed him to consider the more mystical aspects. I needed him to understand he wasn't just challenging historical theories but dangerous and active entities. In the end — to convince him — I had to reveal what I am."

Here she came to a stop, her kit assembled, except for the small pile of broken glass.

"So, what are you, then, exactly?"

Dary gave a wry smile. "Are you familiar with the mythology of Mesopotamia?"

"Not very."

Dary came to sit on the other end of the cot. "If you are going to be an archaeologist, you need to know such myths. Many of the stories humans have relegated to fairy tales have more truth in them than they realise. Modern man seems intent on shrinking his world to something he can look at from all angles, but that means he misses all that lies beyond his narrow scope."

She paused and was slow to speak again, but when she did, each word was hard, bearing the weight of years.

"I don't remember much of my life, but I know I was born human along the banks of the Euphrates. When I was still a child, I was given to a priestess of Tiamat. She took me, and — in newly founded Eridu — trained me in the ways of her goddess. I learned the flow of Unbound Will, what would later be called chaos and entropy. I was just being brought into the secrets of the cult, when Marduk, not yet a god, slew Tiamat. His zealots came to the temple and killed my mistress and her sisters."

My mind was reeling. Eridu was a city founded around the 54th century BCE, and she had been there.

Her eyes glistened, and she flattened a palm against her chest. "I was a young woman with no family, unwelcome in a foreign city, an acolyte to a forsaken god. I had nothing and no one, so when the servants of Lamashtu, the Life-Drinker and Crib-Emptier, came to me, I joined them. What did I owe men that I should say no?"

I didn't know who Lamashtu was, but the terms Life-Drinker and Crib-Emptier screamed bad news. I knew how she might have felt. I had some experience being an orphan in an unfriendly place, and if someone, even someone monstrous, had come to take care of me right when my parents died, I might not have said no.

"I became something other than human, an *edimmu*, a hell-hound of the gallu. Then my memories became mostly useless. Nothing more than a few flashes of thoughts and images, faces and feelings without context. But I know I've done terrible things. The skills I still have are evidence enough of that. It seems there is too much human in me still, and so I can't comprehend the time I've walked this earth, but my body remembers."

She paused for a moment at the power of what she seemed to be recalling, before rocking a little. "I remember meeting Lowe, here in London."

A distant and tearful look came into her eyes. Then something changed, her face somehow becoming sharper, her features more gaunt. Her eyes fluttered, and when her lashes were clear, the tears were replaced by a dangerous gleam. "James is correct. I'm no longer human, but unlike true gallu, I'm not immune to falling in love, like a fool. So, there it is Ibby, the sad and woeful tale of Daria and James. Two hearts separated by demons, aeons and now death. You wouldn't believe it if you hadn't had the past week open your eyes, which is just as well. In this life, denial and ignorance are fatal."

She lapsed into silence, and the gleam left her eyes, but for some time neither of us could find much of anything to say. When I finally did have something to say, the quiet had deepened to something you find in graveyards, churches or libraries.

"So, what happened with Professor Lowe," I began and then cleared my throat. "Ehm, that stuttering and losing focus? That has to do with you?"

Dary nodded, her gaze wandering in the direction Lowe had vanished.

"The spirits of the dead are held by bonds of desire and loyalty. Lowe, like many of your shared bloodline, remains because some part of him cannot surrender his obligation to your bloodline's destiny. This desire and loyalty have kept him from truly departing this life, but when things emerge which disrupt that desire and loyalty, his grip on this world becomes unstable."

I thought of the puzzle box, that last testament to the love lost, and I suddenly felt a sharp pang of sympathy tugging at my heart. After so long, he came face to face with that, and then to have me inadvertently digging up those memories by asking how to solve the puzzle? Poor man.

"So, could your … history with him, be enough to make him disappear forever?"

She nodded again. "The more time we spend together, the more likely that will happen. I need to part ways with both of you. You need his guidance, and he needs to know that the bloodline will not fail."

She rose then, drawing the strap of her kit onto her shoulder. I stood with her, fighting off a flutter of panic.

"Isn't there some way we could coordinate?" I asked, hoping to draw her into conversation and buy myself time to process everything. I'd been drinking from the proverbial firehose and desperately needed time to think things over.

"Not worth the risk," she replied, and headed for the

stairs leading down to the platform. "As James was telling you, this is a long war, and you are going to need him for the duration of it. That way, he can find peace, and you can survive."

"No offence to you or Lowe." I followed a step behind her. "But I think you have a lot more practical experience here. There's no reason you couldn't at least advise from a distance, or be there for backup."

Daria was shaking her head as she began down the stairs.

"No reason besides the one I just gave, and the fact that my saving you has given you the wrong impression. I'm not the good guy here. I did what I did to screw with Sark."

"But you said you were here to help me," I protested, remembering the parking lot. "Why go to so much effort to get me to trust you if all you wanted was to bugger up Dillon's schemes?"

"I could tell you were hurt." She shrugged as she landed on the platform and strode for the tracks. "I needed to make sure you didn't die. You being alive creates a perpetual problem for Dillon and the people holding his leash."

"You still haven't given me anything on those gits," I pointed out, doing my best to keep pace without stepping on her heels. "Seems like an intro to the Wintertherms is in order."

Dary gave a little bark of laughter. "Winterthür," she corrected. "Big, rich and bad — pretty much covers it."

The spectral steam engine came down the tunnel in a cloud of gossamer-threaded smoke, chugging slowly to a stop at the platform. Time was slipping through my fingers.

"At least give me a way to get a hold of you."

Her head shook again, and I had to fight the urge to

pummel nose between those perfect, bouncing locks. Why was she in such a rush?

"That would leave both of us exposed. No offence, Ibby, but you are going to have to step up your covert game before I trust you with anything like that. You were walking around with not one but two naked cells on you. How do you think Sark found you so easily? Oh, that reminds me."

She turned back, drawing my reassembled phone out of her coat.

"I made some adjustments to your phone. It's not perfect, and I'd think twice about using unsecured wi-fi, but you should be able to use it without drawing Winterthür goons like flies to honey."

"What happened to Dillon's phone?" I asked as I took mine.

"Safer for me to have it," Dary replied smoothly and gave me a smile that showed her teeth. "I can use it to make the lives of Sark and a few others much more interesting."

I returned the smile, drawing a wink from Daria, before she turned to board the train. On reflex, I turned the phone on as an inspiration snapped through me.

"Daria," I called as a shiver of hesitation raced through me.

She turned and met my stare. "Yes?" The barest hint of condescension in her tone.

"Can't you just admit that you are leaving because you're sad?"

My phone buzzed, but I ignored it. Dary didn't move, her expression unreadable but her silence far from it.

"Just acknowledge the reason you helped and the reason you are running now have to do with James. I know there's no love lost with Sark, but can we stop pretending that is the only reason you showed up? And while we are at it, let's be clear that you aren't leaving now to keep James safe."

Her face twitched with something like a snarl, and those leonine teeth showed. "Didn't I say I was leaving to protect him?"

"You did." I nodded, taking a step closer and ignoring another buzz from my phone. "But we both know that is bollocks. Lowe's been strong enough to hold it together with your memory for a century. He can manage now. The real reason is that *you* don't want to remember *him*. You want to forget so you don't have to hurt anymore, and you are so set on that, you'll leave James and I in a state to do it."

Daria's expression remained stony for a heartbeat, before it cracked into a deprecating smile.

"You got me, kid." She shrugged and slid a step back into the train. "What can I say? Not a good guy."

My phone buzzed for a third time, and with an angry huff, I looked down.

My heart stopped. My mouth went dry, which was just as well because I was seconds from dropping to all fours and retching brokenly on the deck of the platform.

"What are you playing at?" Dary asked suspiciously. "You going to pretend like you still need doctoring to get me to stay?"

Words wouldn't come, so I held up the phone. Daria rolled her eyes and stepped forwards to take it.

"I hope you aren't planning something stupid," she muttered as she raised the screen to her eyes. "Because then you really will need a doctor …"

Dary's eyes widened, and she looked at me and then looked back to the phone. "Who's that?"

"Jackie," I managed to gasp. "He's got my best friend."

Chapter Nineteen

I couldn't stop seeing the cruel bruises on her creamy complexion, the crusted trickle of blood from her nose, the tears welling in her red-rimmed eyes. Every detail filled me with a righteous fury. I drew it in with each breath, and when I needed an ignition point for the rage, I directed my recollection to the text headlining the photo.

FOR SALE: ONE USED SLUT, TWO RINGS PER UNIT, LIMITED TIME OFFER

My hands curled into fists, the knuckles popped. The rings responded to my anger, stretching my sense far and wide. I became aware of every piece of metal around me for dozens of metres, and that awareness was like a tactile connection, a cord of implied command. I was a master puppeteer with a thousand strings, waiting to make tiny rivets and huge steel girders dance to my boiling whim.

It was a heady and empowering sensation, but it was making it difficult to focus.

"Ibby," a voice intruded on my brooding. "Ibby, did you hear me?"

No. No, I hadn't. I was struggling to find a reason to care. I was going to rip the entire rotten city in two, shake it until either my friend or Dillon came loose. What more was there to discuss?

"Ibukun Bashir!" someone else snapped, catching me like a hook.

"What?" I snarled, crashing back to the world as my eyes opened. I hadn't even realised I'd closed them.

Lowe and Dary eyed me warily, still in the station commons. I was about to demand what they wanted when a bench floated past.

Several objects had taken up a slow orbit with me as the nexus. Iron benches and brass stanchions drifted in lazy circles, responding to the storm of my emotions.

"Sorry," I muttered and then did my best to set the furnishings on the floor. A chorus of bumps and scrapes echoed in the station as they settled into a rough semi-circle behind me.

"I'm listening," I promised, pushing back the seductive thoughts of vengeance. I needed to be present, or I wasn't going to be much use to my friend.

Dary gave me a warning look. "Like I was saying, Sark, for all his blustering innuendo, is not going to throw away his best bargaining chip. As we can see from the text, he's not above getting a little rough with her, but he needs to keep her alive to draw you in."

I felt the anger surge up inside me, and before I knew exactly what was happening, words were ripping from my tongue.

"That bargaining chip is named Jackie Davies, and she looks absolutely terrified. We need to consider he's being more than just a little rough with her."

"You're not helping," Daria replied, her expression throwing ice water on my smouldering temper. "Blind rage will only make you stupid. That's why Sark sent the photo. He wants you angry and desperate. Don't give that bastard what he wants."

Lowe was nodding. "Daria's correct. As difficult as it is, we need to remember someone like this Dillon Sark is a scoundrel and preys on the feelings of others."

"I know," I growled. "I know. Again, sorry. I just hate that I've only been at this a few days, and it's managed to destroy every aspect of my life and those I care about."

"Miss Davies isn't beyond help." Lowe placed a hand on my shoulder. "If we plan accordingly, we can make sure she's safe."

I nodded and looked at Dary, who was holding my phone, one thumb punching away. My heart caught in my chest, and I slipped out from under Lowe's reassuring grip.

"Has he sent anything else?"

"No," she replied as she finished with a final tap to the screen. "I'm asking him where he wants to make the trade. We have a minute or two while he tries to trace our position, but with the changes I made, he'll give up on that quickly. He's always been too impatient."

It was like playing chess, except in this game, I didn't know which pieces Sark had or how many. Dary seemed to have a good grasp of how Dillon operated, but even she was only going on intuition and character judgements.

"How long have you known Dillon?" I asked, curious at her seemingly extensive knowledge of a man who'd so quickly gone from shady best friend's boyfriend to enemy mastermind. "Last I knew he was a student at the university." An unpleasant thought popped into my mind. "He's not a hell-hound, like …"

"Like me," Dary finished. "No, Dillon is plain old

human evil, just not so young as he presents. He's put on this façade half a dozen times. An independently wealthy, handsome student of one stripe or another. He keeps it up for a few years, never more than five, gathering information and ruining lives before slinking away. Six months to a year later, he resurfaces with a new cover, often including a cosmetically altered face."

He was a chameleon, with all the cold-blooded ruthlessness that implied. The image of some reptilian thing peeling off a mask like Dillon's soulful, bad boy face came to mind, and I suppressed a shudder.

"He has to know his cover can't last," Lowe wondered aloud. "He'll be caught eventually, by those who recognise him, even if he does look different."

"I don't doubt it." Dary nodded. "But you'd be amazed what gets swept under the rug. Winterthür has ambitions they'll kill for, but most institutions are less dangerous only because their ambitions are smaller. Dillon has been working this theatre for long enough, and he has enough contacts who could insulate him from accusations. But given what his goal is, I doubt he cares about that."

"What's his goal, though?" I asked. "I get that Dillon wants the rings, and that it has something to do with that Kezsarak thing. But do we know anything beyond that? I mean, I don't want to give him anything, but this is a woman's life we are talking about. What is going to happen if I show up, toss him the rings and take Jackie?"

Lowe shook his head sharply, dismissing the suggestion, while Dary's eyes widened.

"This rogue can't be trusted to keep his word," Lowe stated. "Once he has what he wants, you both become nothing more than loose ends he will tie off as expediently as possible. We can't just give him the rings."

"Kezsarak," Dary said carefully as though she was

afraid it might burn her tongue. "How do you know this has to do with Kezsarak?"

I pointed at Lowe. Under the spotlight, he sputtered for a moment and adjusted his spectacles.

"W-well, I suppose I don't know anything for a-absolute certain, at least not until one of us sees his prison, but all the s-signs are there that he is near."

"What signs?" Dary asked sharply.

"Most of it has to do with Ibby. She has come under psychic assault, manifesting as nightmares, multiple times over the past several days, twice in my presence. Her nightmares smell of 'gallu,' but there is a distinct difference between what she is experiencing and the spoor of lesser demons. And there was the ash."

"Ash?" Dary's expression took on an inscrutable interest. Was that fear or excitement sparkling in her eyes?

I tasted a phantom of the acrid stuff at the back of my throat. "A couple of times, I coughed up ash. It was like a chimney-sweep convention down here."

Dary's eyes held a ferocious glint. "This is perfect," she said in a husky purr. "Really, it couldn't be more perfect."

Lowe and I shared a confused look.

"Winterthür, among many other things, are on the hunt for ways to access and control the powers of the ancients. Kezsarak's Cask is no different than other such pursuits, except for one point: they need an Inconquo with the rings to release the poor demon. That's where our advantage lies."

I caught hard on the 'poor demon' point, and was struggling to form a reply when Lowe leapt into the fray.

"You are not seriously suggesting that she cooperate with these blaggards! What that brute did to Ibby earns nothing but a punched ticket to Ol' Scratch, not capitulation! And since when did unleashing ancient demons become an option!"

A breeze I couldn't feel ruffled Lowe's clothes. The temperature dropped several degrees.

"What I am suggesting," Dary replied, "is that there is a good chance Sark wants not just the rings, but Ibby too. If that is the case, then we need to capitalise on that. Before anything else, Sark is going to protect himself. That includes accomplishing his mission. I don't doubt Winterthür is already pressuring him to wrap up this messy business, and so if Ibby at least presents the front of cooperation, he has incentive to take her at face value."

Before anyone else could argue the phone buzzed, and Dary automatically opened the message and read aloud.

"South Greenwich Foundry, East Industrial. Both sets of rings, two hours or Jackie eats a bullet."

My knees felt weak, and I gulped.

Greenwich was less than twenty minutes by tube from central London, but I'd never had much reason to go there.

"Are either of you familiar with the place?" I asked.

Lowe shook his head, but Daria was nodding, and she was using my phone to look something up.

"Yes," she said distractedly. "I've actually been there a few times, as it is one of Sark's preferred spots to do business. Here, you can see why."

She showed me several aerial photos of a derelict industrial area. Rusty stitches of defunct rail lines traced a path to a cluster of crumbling buildings in the middle of a vast lot of cracked pavement, mud and piles of twisted debris. There was nothing green within hundreds of metres of the place. Only ugly brown creepers seemed capable of penetrating the crushing, industrial refuse.

Cycling through the images, I found an interior photo

with a grainy texture of age. Several potbellied vats suspended by chains hung over a dark hall, a snarled-up assembly track running its length. A man in a hard hat stood under the slag-streaked vats, the only suggestion of human scale. Each vat looked to be the size of a lorry.

"It's definitely desolate," I observed. "I imagine it doesn't get much traffic."

"It's a dead spot in more ways than one," Dary explained, clicking a nail on the screen. "You could use the place as a shooting range and never have to worry about the authorities. If you tried to make a call with anything less than a military grade satellite phone, you'd just drain your battery."

"Wow." London was a wi-fi soup. If this place was a dead zone, then it really was the middle of nowhere.

"You're going to need to get going. The nearest station is still a long walk. He's not going to wait for a confirmation that you received the message. In two hours, you're there or your friend is dead."

Reality so baldly stated was like a kick in the stomach. Though I wanted to curl into the foetal position, I settled for bracing my hands on my hips. I took a few slow breaths, gathering my thoughts and my nerve.

Lowe interjected a thought that had occurred to me multiple times throughout this conversation. "How do we know that they plan to keep Ibby alive? Not to be indelicate, but couldn't they just shoot her dead and take the rings? They murdered me easily enough."

"Possible, but unlikely," replied Daria. "On two counts: first, they didn't immediately do that when they ambushed her outside the university. Sark beat her, and one of his goons lost control at the end, but if they'd wanted her dead, Ibby would've been bleeding out on the pavement before she knew they were there."

It was hard to remember everything from my last encounter with Dillon, but the moment when the big thug stood over me with his pistol flashed in my mind.

"… Hang Sark's orders."

The statement gave some credence to Dary's theory.

"The second thing is while the Inconquo bloodline has obviously spread," Dary said as she pointed to me and Lowe with each hand. "It's very diluted. You, James, had just enough to draw you to the rings, but you never could have exerted the power and control Ibby has already displayed. They are not going to waste a chance to control the bloodline."

"What do you mean 'control the bloodline'?" I asked.

Lowe shuffled his feet and looked embarrassed.

"Depending on the father's parentage, your children could be just as strong in the blood as you," Daria explained. "So Winterthür will make sure they find a suitable match, and then … they will make sure you keep having children."

"Oh …" I breathed as the reality of the stakes was driven home.

It was a struggle to meet Lowe's mournful gaze. "I'm sorry, Ibby, truly. If I'd known … if I could help … if …"

I shook my head and took his hand.

"Hey." I forced a smile and shrugged. "This is the family business, right?"

Lowe's grin was no less an act of will as my own, but there was a sincerity we both understood regardless.

IT IS A PECULIAR THING, putting your affairs in order.

The odds seemed stacked against me. So, I decided to spend my last sliver of time saying goodbye as best I could.

An email apiece to Meredith and Professor Schottelkirk, apologising for the 'complications' I'd brought on them and thanking them for what they had been to me. I also sent one to Markus, unable to shake how nice it was he'd covered for me, not just once when he went looking for Lowe, but also when he thought I'd tricked him.

I wrote something to Jackie. If she survived, she'd know what she'd meant to a girl who'd felt so alone for so long.

I managed to make it through all of that without surrendering to tears, but now I was on what might be my final message to Uncle Iry, and I couldn't hold it back anymore. Tears rolled down my cheeks, and I had to pause to clear my eyes.

I couldn't possibly tell him all the ways I loved him and appreciated what he'd done. Sometimes, words are too small, but the small things make all the difference.

As I wiped my eyes for the last time, I read over what I wrote to Iry just once. A second time, and I'd never get on the train out of Museum Station.

DEAR UNCLE IRY, *a'am in my heart of hearts,*

I may not be able to answer your messages when you have time to reach out, but I wanted to let you know that I love and miss you.

When mother and father were taken, I felt so alone and so small. I was as lost as I'd ever been. I was crippled by the grief, so I thought I would never be able to live. It hurt too much.

But you would not let me stay that way.

You called me and sent messages every day. Sometimes, twice a day, no matter what it cost you. When you could barely feed yourself, you were bartering whatever you had to keep in touch with me. Why you would do that for a child you never touched, never held or even saw in the flesh is beyond me. You dragged me out of the pit and brought light and hope back into my life.

You saved me, a'am, and I know why. We are family, and that is something which distance and circumstance can't change.

Family, eayila, and because of my family, I am going to do something my loved ones taught me.

Did father ever tell you what to do when the world gets ugly? You live it every day, so I know you do.

Make it better by being better.

That is what I'm trying for, and I hope you'll be proud. Don't worry about me, and take care of yourself.

Love,

Ibby

Chapter Twenty

Dary promised to ride with me to Greenwich Pier, but beyond that, I was on my own. She smiled as she reminded me she was 'still not a good guy,' but I couldn't help thinking there was a pain in her expression that had nothing to do with her bandaged arm.

From the Pier, I had Dary's directions and my phone's GPS to get me to the gates of the foundry complex. I'd have to take it at a trot.

I sat watching the thickening grey of the skies through the window, willing the train to go faster. Then I felt something give a little wobble in the train's undercarriage, and I decided an Inconquo willing a high-speed train to do anything was not in anyone's best interests.

I slumped in my seat and looked out over the car. It was filled with workaday types. Many of them were on their phones. Several others wore earbuds. Three had their noses in a book, while one chap was knitting and humming. A handful sat and stared at the floor or out the window, looking forlorn.

Despite the crowds, Dary and I seemed to find the one

spot where we had some breathing room from the mass of frowning faces and shuffling feet. This was just as well, because as my eyes fell on Dary, the storm of conflicting thoughts and emotions emerged. I wanted to ask her about things I'd rather not have overheard.

I was under no illusions she would be waiting for me to return. This might be the last time I saw her, even if I survived the night. A few answers might make the difference between life and death when facing Sark and possibly Kezsarak.

"Is there something you want to say to me, Ibby?" she asked, as if she could read my mind.

I realised I had been staring at her, so it was little wonder she'd asked the question.

"Yeah," I grunted, my mind shuffling thoughts in line like notecards.

Dary peaked an eyebrow. She swept her uninjured hand before her in a grand gesture, signalling me to continue.

"Sorry, there's been so much in such a short time I hardly know where to start." I met her curious stare with a forcibly steady gaze. "We've been talking a lot about demons or gallu, and while I'm not going to deny that something seems to be coming after me in my dreams, I'm having a hard time believing that evil spirits are everywhere, giving people excuses for the terrible things they do. In my experience, people don't need a little devil on their shoulder to be wicked."

Dary paused for a second to see if I was done, and then she pursed her lips as she nodded.

"You are right that the vast majority of terrible things and almost all the historically significant events have happened because mortals have been wretched. Typically, gallu try to avoid such things because it would threaten the greatest tool they ever devised to protect them and isolate their enemies."

The implied conspiracy, some ancient scheme between wilful, inhuman forces sent prickles down my spine. My hair was starting to stand on end.

"What tool?"

"Unbelief," Dary said. "Imagine how easy it is to hide when everyone is actively denying you exist. Not only will people consider it implausible to suspect a demon as the cause of a crime, but anyone who suggests it is punished with social censure. For the past few centuries, in the civilised world, gallu have had to do very little to cover their tracks, since humans do it for them in the name of being reasonable."

The grin that had settled on her features was all the more chilling for the beautiful features it hung on. I think she saw my growing discomfort because the smile quickly dissolved, and her face took on a conciliatory aspect.

"Though, it's worth mentioning that many gallu only use disbelief as a cover to be left alone. It works well as a sword to cut off those that come looking, but more often it is a shield to hide under. Almost as many gallu, unable to change with the times, just want to live out their immortal existence without fear."

"When talking about Winterthür's plan to control Kezsarak, you said 'poor demon.' What did you mean?"

Daria didn't answer immediately, instead she stared out the window where clouds stole the beauty of the setting sun. "Kezsarak's story is a sad one. One that lies at the root of the Inconquo. My mistress in the temple of Tiamat told me. I kept it close to my heart because it has to do with how I came to serve at the temple."

I scooted to the edge of my seat. Dary warmed to her story and drew closer to me as well. I'm sure we looked like two besties sharing juicy gossip. Her voice was low and clear, her eyes fixed on mine.

"During that time, the line between man, hero and god was thin, and the gallu moved openly among men. Some were worshipped and some feared. The first great cities had erected their strong walls less than a century before, and the world seemed headed towards a new, bright age. But that was when Asag came."

The name made me shiver a little, and I crossed my arms. "Asag?"

"Asag was the greatest, most terrible and powerful gallu ever whispered about. Aside from his awful power, he brought his children: rock-skinned demons, the result of his ravaging of mountain spirits. They fell upon the first cities. Many of them were destroyed, their people slaughtered, because Asag hated and feared mankind. He poisoned the land and waters. Even those not in the great cities suffered and died. That was why my parents gave me to Tiamat's service. They hoped the cult would see me through the famine. I survived, but my mother and father were not so lucky."

I felt like I should reach out and take her hand, share, in some small way, the burden of her pain.

"Gods and heroes were beaten back. All seemed lost until one night when Kezsarak came to the camp of Ninurta, the last of those who fought Asag. Kezsarak was Asag's child, but he had stayed in the mountains as he'd always done, not taking part in the destruction. Instead, he learned the secrets of the ores of his mother. Some of these, he shared with men, but he kept others to himself. He shared one such secret to save mankind, whom he loved for the beautiful things they could make. He taught Ninurta how to make a cage to hold his father and siblings, and then he returned to the mountains."

I struggled to connect this beneficent hermit with the terrible presence that haunted my dreams, but I didn't interrupt.

"Asag, catching wind of Kezsarak's alliance, found his son and beat a confession from him. Kezsarak swore he only wanted peace, that men only had the power to bind gallu, not destroy them. It didn't matter because Ninurta used Kezsarak's secret and fashioned a weapon, not a cage, Sharur the Smasher of Thousands. With this weapon, he struck down Asag. His father died cursing his son's betrayal. Kezsarak, stunned and broken at Ninurta's betrayal, lived to see his siblings slaughtered by the weapon Ninurta made with the secrets Kezsarak had given him."

"That's … horrible," I said quietly.

Dary nodded. "The blight of Asag ended, and Ninurta was a hero, but Kezsarak declared men murderers. He retreated to the mountains."

"But, he didn't stay there?"

Dary shook her head and then gave a shrug. "No, but the next part of the story I don't know as well. I had already entered the service of Lamashtu when Kezsarak returned to plague mankind, so my knowledge is based in what I've read and what Lowe taught me, which is pretty murky, frankly."

Outside, the leaden clouds were making good on their brooding promise, spitting heavy drops. Over Greenwich, the storm was thicker. The clouds congealed into a deep, weeping bruise.

Dary's voice drew my gaze back.

"Kezsarak returned and spoke to the tools of men, made them instruments of destruction unlike anything man had seen. Workmen were maimed, buildings fell and battles became slaughters where none survived. The people asked for help, and though Ninurta was gone, his descendants, who'd written the ancient voice of metals into their bones, came forwards to correct their ancestors' mistake."

Inconquo, I thought. *It always comes back to family.*

"Because Kezsarak had been betrayed by Ninurta, the Inconquo resolved not to kill him, but to bind him. That is why they made the rings. Rings bind things, physically as well as metaphorically. The rings of the Inconquo were made to bind Kezsarak. It is only with them that he can be unbound. Thousands of years ago, the Inconquo took on the mantle of guardians when they first bound Kezsarak. You get to start the same way."

"Why would they want to free something as destructive and uncontrollable as Kezsarak?"

Dary gazed out the window at the passing landscape. "Mortals long for power, to shape the world to suit them. They'll do terrible things to get that power. It falls to those like us to tell them, forcefully, when they are being fools."

I smiled at that, but it was mostly to hide the churning I felt in my stomach. A voice signalled we were minutes out from Greenwich. I was going to be out in that pelting rain, racing towards an abandoned industrial complex, meeting with a monster of a man who had a plan to unleash a real monster.

I closed my eyes and felt the car around me — the rail beneath me, the lines above me and the brush of metallic songs against my mind. Each tingled psychically as they flew by, each offering a passing oath of fealty. Ready to serve, ready to fight.

It was a power inherited by my family from long ago, but it was more than that.

I possessed a gift now that was more frightening and powerful than anything I could have imagined. With that ability came an implicit purpose. Now, I had the chance to honour that purpose, not just by stopping those who would abuse it, but by protecting a friend who was now in danger.

Family is about responsibility, and responsibility flows both ways.

I knew what I had to do.

When I opened my eyes and met Daria's gaze, she straightened. The gleam sprang back into her eyes, and she nodded slowly.

The automated voice came on again as the train slowed.

I found a grim smile that felt dangerous. I was an Inconquo, and I was going to war.

Chapter Twenty-One

I didn't end up needing my phone to find the meeting place, which was just as well, because manipulating a touch screen in pelting rain was a challenge.

I'd left Dary at Greenwich Pier, giving her a squeeze before heading out into the rain. Cold drops struck my face as I trotted along, though my pilfered leather jacket took the brunt of the abuse. By the time I reached the foundry, I'd be soaked.

I trotted down King William Walk, trainers slapping in the rain until I reached Greenwich Theatre and the Statue of William the Fourth on his grey plinth. Passing beneath the venerable king's gaze, I looked for the break in the hedge that would let me slip under the line of trees leading into Greenwich Park. It was south by southeast from there through the forest to the foundry fence.

The going was mostly flat, and even when moving over the slick carpet of heaven-watered grass, my steps were steady and unfaltering. The storm gave a low growl, and the sound sparked a heady rush of adrenaline.

My chest heaving and every limb twitching with

energy, I passed through a dense line of trees to emerge on a scruffy field. In the centre of this barren expanse was a collection of rusty buildings, which were wrapped in a sagging chain link fence.

It struck me as strange to find an establishment of heavy industry squatting at the base of a park, but much of this area — once connected to the Thames by rail — had been used for this purpose. Only after the blitz when so much was already demolished, the industrial area was cleared and the slow transformation into a park began. The foundry had been a last holdout. Fears of heavy metals released into the burgeoning park complicated its demolition, and so it remained an ugly reminder of what all these acres of land had once been.

I slowed to a walk, letting my metallic sense stretch wide. Every hair felt stiff in anticipation. Dillon had called me here to make a trade. If he wanted to, he could have a sharpshooter strike me where I stood.

Why was I thinking about snipers? I needed to keep my nerve. Jackie needed me.

There was a gate set into the fence, or what was left of one. One hinged panel hung haphazardly while the other was lying flat on the gravelly ground. Beyond that stood a small guard house, which was now little more than disintegrating planks. The last sentries watched over a wide crushed-rock path that stretched between low rectangular buildings, their paint long stripped away to reveal vast sheets of corroded tin. Past these flanking buildings stood the foundry itself. A swollen, many-storeyed hulk of concrete, whose rusting steel bones were beginning to show through its grey hide. One of the three-storey-tall bay doors yawned open like a toothless mouth.

"Into the belly of the beast," I muttered as I eased my

way through the broken gate, mindful of the barbed wire that hung in snarled-up clumps.

My feet crunched on the gravel as I walked down the lane between the paired garage bays, the sound of rain on the roof terribly loud. I felt a peculiar itch between my shoulder blades as I went between the two buildings. My subconscious was determined to use my body to tell me things I already knew. I knew I was being watched, and more than likely, they had a gun trained on me as I was walking up to the gate. I fought to keep from hunching down because the next step would be rushing for cover, and a sudden move like that could mean not only my death but Jackie's as well.

"They want you alive," Dary had explained back at the Pier. "But they're not going to risk losing the rings. Better a dead you and half the rings than no rings — is how they'll see it."

I was gunning for a live me and no rings for them, but I also needed Jackie alive, so right now, it was a high wire act. One foot in front of the other.

The walls of the building were vast, crumbling and pockmarked expanses of grey, darkened by the rain with dangling stretches of moss.

I moved up the stairway, letting my metallic sense tell me where the rusty metal could still bear my weight. My eyes remained fixed on the double doors with their cracked, wired windows as my mind's eye guided my every step up the stairs.

The stair groaned, and I could feel the strain stretching all the way to the decrepit bolts and down the metal shafts set in the ground.

I stepped to the doors, and now standing level with them, I saw they were not only unlocked but also ajar. I cautiously drew one open. Inside was a tiled hallway.

Debris lay in cast-off drifts, and the walls were a leprous expanse of flaking paint. Impossibly, at the far end of the hallway, a single lightbulb burned over a sign set above double doors.

"They left the light on for me," I said, chuckling and immediately regretted it as my voice echoed down the corridor. I cast one look over my shoulder, hoping I'd be walking or perhaps running back this way soon. The alternative wasn't worth contemplating.

Inside, the air seemed to thicken in my lungs, and the smell and taste of iron in the air — deadened by the rain outside — was invasively ever present. Avoiding the piles of rubbish, I tried not to look too hard down the dark side passages.

I stopped under that lightbulb and read the sign over the doors, my hair and clothes dripping.

WARNING
MOLTEN METAL AND POISONOUS GAS
AUTHORISED PERSONNEL ONLY

Beneath the sign, one of the doors had been worked over by a graffiti artist of considerably more skill than the others who had decorated the locale. A stylised depiction of a man in a gas mask took up the window, a sinister industrial ghoul keeping watch. Beneath the blind sentry were scrawled lyrics, whose style mimicked the lines and shapes of the picture above. I read them as my fingers slowly came to rest on the opposite door:

She's from Birmingham! BAM-BA-LAM
Up there in Anglo-lan! BAM-BA-LAM
Well, she's bangin' that thing! BAM-BA-LAM
Boy, makes me ears ring! BAM-BA-LAM

Can't feel me bones roast! BAM-BA-LAM
Don't know I'm a ghost! BAM-BA-LAM

Not as ominous as 'Abandon all hope …' but it certainly didn't fill a soul with confidence.

Just beyond the doors, I thought I could hear the sounds of low voices.

I quieted my last doubts and stilled the tremble in my hand.

THE DOORS LED onto the foundry floor and there — lined with rails and beneath the looming weight of huge buckets — stood a man next to a kneeling woman. They were backlit by a pair of tripod-mounted work lights. Behind them, the rails and buckets stretched out into the dark. No one else was in sight, but an army complete with armoured vehicles could have fit in the expanse of dark space behind them.

I stretched my sense of the metallic out and found myself slammed with resonance. Everything was metal. Floor, walls, rails, buckets, the ceiling high above, even traces of the stuff were in the air. Panic quickened my breath as I fought to reorient myself.

I took a few faltering steps, pushing the auras into categories in rapid succession.

"Jackie, you okay?" I called. I needed to buy time.

My vision blurred from the assault on my mind, but it cleared enough for me to watch Jackie struggle to rise up off her knees. Her hands were bound, and her movements were stiff. The man next to her sent her to the ground with a shove, and a sob of pain echoed through the cavernous space.

I hissed, anger giving me greater focus and the momentum to rush forwards several steps. "Leave her alone."

"Do you have the rings?" the man shouted. It was Dillon.

I held up the two ring-bearing fingers in a rude gesture. "What do you think, tosspot!"

Something tickled at the back of my mind. Metals different than the amalgams I was sensing from the static foundry shifted behind me.

"I think I win," Dillon laughed.

I whipped around swinging the rings in a wide, looping punch. My vision caught up as one wiry man collided into another. Both held cattle prods, which sparked and crackled as they floundered on the ground. It might have been hilarious if I wasn't given a first-hand introduction to what they were feeling.

There was a third cattle prod. I hadn't distinguished it from the cloud of metallic auras, and it took me squarely in the back.

Pain, brilliant and mind blasting, danced along my nerves, forcing muscles to clench violently. My world became a senseless white glare, except that I hurt everywhere, inside and out. Even after the current left me, my body shook and nerves sizzled.

The first thing that came back to any semblance of order was my metallic sense, and I realised with desperate urgency that the pronged pain-stick still hovered over me. Faster than rational thought, I sent it reeling away. It moved at the speed of a blink, taking the clenching hand with it. The man followed after with a cry. A dull wet thunk, like a branch popping free of a tree, and then screaming.

I hadn't realised I was on all fours and scrambled to my

feet. Tottering on cramping legs, I felt the other two cattle prods, and threw my will at them, twisting until their casings cracked and handles shivered. I had a moment of grim satisfaction before I realised with horror that the two men had cast aside their weapons and were circling me now with nothing but clenched fists and hate-filled eyes.

My mind swept over them, but I couldn't sense any metal. They were learning.

As the first one closed, I thought to use the aluminium panelling of the floor, but the aftershock of the cattle prod made focusing difficult. I managed to crumple it up enough to trip the man coming for me. If my legs had worked properly, I might've gotten out of his way. Instead, he barrelled into me, shoulder down like a junior rugby star, knocking me clean off my feet.

Air erupted from my lungs as his driving shoulder slammed me into the floor. There was a squelch of wet clothing and my bruised ribs threw up a chorus of agonised protests. The tackler's feet were still pumping, scuffing at the floor, driving me down and back even as I tried to worm away.

My lungs fought to re-inflate, but his crushing weight smothered me as my mouth gaped like a suffocating fish.

I felt the tension in his muscles just before he threw his weight to one side, trying to pin me down. In a flash of inspiration, I twisted my hips and shoved against the ground with my hands and feet, using his momentum and repelling against the metal panels beneath me to send him flying. His shoulder struck the floor like a gong, and he staggered long enough for me to climb to my feet.

I drew in my first full breath of air as I straightened, making it two steps before I was grabbed from behind, my arms pinned behind my back. I screamed and tried to throw my head back to head-butt him, but he used my imbalance to drive me to the floor. My shoulder and one cheek took the impact, but his tight grip actually stabilised me enough that I kept my teeth.

One hand pinched my wrists together, hard enough to draw a hiss, and a second later, I felt him trying to loop something over my wrists. I thrashed and bucked, but his grip was vicelike, and he was leveraging his greater weight. I tried to rise up, but he drove me down, harder this time. My jaw bounced off the floor and my teeth clacked together.

The thought of teeth struck me. My scrambled metallic perception filtered through waves of fatigue and warbling metal auras until I found what I'd hoped for.

Inside his mouth.

With ferocious glee, I pulled hard at the metal filling in his jaw. I heard as well as felt the telltale zip of a plastic cable tie tightening. The edge of the restraint bit into my wrists a second before the man fell off me with a muffled scream. My hands bound together behind my back, it was a chore to get to my knees, where I could see his face in the glare of the work lights. Jaw clenching, I twisted the filling viciously.

His hands pawed at his mouth, and with a cry of pain from him, the filling came free.

I was about to drive the little kernel of metal down his throat, but my world rocked under a blunt impact across the back of my skull. My desperate fight seemed a paltry distraction to the need to lie down, and thankfully the earth rose up to greet me.

I lay there for a time, seeing but not seeing, hearing but not hearing, feeling but not feeling as the world rolled by. I heard voices, but the words warbled as though under water, as waves pounded against my eardrums. Only once my brain registered the thudding in my ears was my own heart, I realised that something might be wrong.

Should it really be that loud? I thought, and after hearing another beat, the absurd thought bubbled up. *Maybe I should ask someone for help.*

I recalled that hands had been moving me, dragging me around and someone tugged something from my fingers. I had the briefest feeling of deep anxiety and terrible anger at the separation, but it was gone before I could understand why I was so upset.

An ugly smile split the handsome face hovering just in front of me.

Maybe he can help me, I thought, but another look at his face provoked a deep distrust and sense of outrage.

Dillon's leering countenance materialised from the face in front of me. I was coming to my senses, and my senses hurt. My head, back, shoulder, and most awfully, my ribs demanded I acknowledge their pain. NOW.

My concussion-addled brain wasn't having any of that, so instead I took stock of the mess I'd wakened to find myself in.

At some point, I'd been dragged closer to the light, and now sat, my arms behind me, next to a form I recognised as Jackie's. She was gagged, bound and hobbled, and lay on the stained filing-flecked floor where Dillon had left her. Her doe eyes were huge with terror as she looked at me and everything else at once. For all her feminine beauty, she reminded me of a twitching rabbit caught in a snare. My heart ached for her.

Dillon grabbed my hair, pushing my head back and forcing me to look at his face.

"I suppose I should've expected something so brave and stupid from the likes of you, but you are always impressive to watch. I don't imagine you'll be nearly so sporting without these," he said, chuckling, as he held up something in front of my face.

My stomach twisted, and my heart spasmed. I recognised the diamond-shaped pattern of pale ore set in cuneiformed copper. With my hands bound together behind my back, I realised it was true: Dillon had all four of the rings now!

But he still needed me to open Kezsarak's prison. That thought kept me from collapsing, and as I looked up into Dillon's smug face, I knew I'd die before I did that. That realisation dragged my eyes down to Jackie. Even for her sake, I wouldn't open that prison. I didn't know how to communicate that to her, but I caught her eye and I gave her an encouraging nod. Just because we were both unlikely to make it out of here in one piece didn't mean that she had to go out feeling alone, scared and helpless.

A hard hand pinched my cheeks and twisted my face up and around.

"I want to make sure you don't miss this," Dillon said.

I growled and snapped my teeth, but his hand retreated and then backhanded me across the cheek. I felt skin split under the hard blow, and I realised he already had two of the rings on his hand.

"That's not very nice," he chided and rose from his crouch. "Behave yourself, or I'll have to get creative."

As a point of emphasis, he planted his heel on Jackie's fingers when he stood and ground down as he rose. Jackie barely stirred from her frightened stupor enough to give a mewling sob until the foot came away.

"Now watch this," he said, hissing, while he fit the second pair of rings beside the first. When he was done, the raised knuckles of the rings formed a bar across the fist, like a full set of brass knuckles. His fingers flexed, and the rings clicked against each other as he savoured the sight.

Was he just showing off? I couldn't be sure, but I either way I was grateful. Though it was harder without the rings, I was beginning to work at an expanse of rail. The binding screws and nails were coming loose from the tracks near the work light, all for use against the goons spread about the foundry hall. For Dillon, I concocted something unique involving a section of rail and a constricting squeeze.

"I wouldn't do that if I were you."

Dillon didn't look up from basking in the rings' luminous glimmerings in the stark white light. My mental efforts with the screws slowed to a stop. Could he see what I was doing? I was doing it to a length of rail that stretched behind him. Had he heard a squeak of protesting screws or something?

Unsure, but refusing to give up on my plan, I went back to moving things into place.

I felt a ripple of disturbance in the auras I was manipulating, and then there was an incredible force which ripped the rail section out of my grip. I watched in shock as the rail twisted up like a charmed snake, rising behind Dillon and then slithering forwards to sway by his side.

"You're not the only one with tricks, cuz," Dillon observed flatly, and then the metal python struck.

Chapter Twenty-Two

The iron snake wound around my body, holding me fast as I lay on my side like one of those unappetising hors d'oeuvres: the pig-in-a-blanket. The rust-dusted metal was painfully tight, bruising my thighs, back and arms. I closed my eyes to tune its song to my mind, but a sharper command cut through. The coiled metal squeezed a little more in response, and I gasped.

"No more of that, sweety," Dillon chided. "I've got plans for you. You give me trouble, and the sun will rise on one less Inconquo tomorrow."

My eyes flew open as I made a connection. *Dillon is Inconquo.*

Winterthür had spent decades looking for the rings. Of course, the agent they used was Inconquo. How could I not have guessed?

I hung my head, defeat weighing like a crown of lead. Jackie lay on the ground nearby, bound and foetal, her red-rimmed eyes and battered face staring up. Hope was gone from her expression. I'd failed her and without much of a fight.

"I'm sorry, Jackie," I said softly. "I tried."

Jackie just blinked at me until Dillon drew closer, then she curled in on herself. A moan escaped her throat.

"Now, you be quiet and watch the show," Dillon said, stooping to pat my head before lifting his voice to someone in the dark. "Lights up! Let's bring out our next guest!"

The overhead lights, framed in heavy cages of wire, came to life, each one burning a dull mustard shade before rallying to full fluorescent life. These miniature industrial suns dawned the length of the hall. The buckets hanging from chains were rigged to overhead gears and tracks. They ran the space in two parallel lines, passing over wide vats recessed in the floor. Steel-sided carts sat mouldering on the rails, and a few scabby-flanked lorries had died in the middle of the floor.

Dillon's men — more of them now — stood at a foldout plastic table. Several dark forms lay there, but at the centre was a single cube.

An icy claw seized my heart. I'd never seen the cube before, but I knew what it was. Kezsarak's Cask. My nightmares dragged themselves from my subconscious. I could hear 'the voice,' whether it was memory or a fresh assault.

YESSS.

Dillon's thugs came over and began to drag-carry Jackie and me towards the table.

I writhed, but the coil pinned me from shoulder to mid-thigh, so I only managed to throw myself on the floor twice. Each impact jarred my bandaged ribs against the rail and squeezed a cry of pain from me. Then hands hauled me up to drag me towards the cube again.

I was breathless with pain and exhaustion by the time Jackie and I were deposited near the table, where Dillon now stood.

A cornucopia of firearms lay on the table like some

macabre street merchant's display. Handguns like the ones I'd seen the thugs use and tactical carbines that police officers carried. Multiple shotguns, one with its barrel cut down to a finger length. Shells and magazines sitting by each.

Dominating the display was the cube, a miniature idol keeping watch over this offering of violence. Constructed of intersecting and overlapping bands of metal, each one different, not just by colour but by their resonance. Each band was etched with a strand of cuneiform. Though the cube looked dingy and worn with age, each glyph was sharply defined and looked fresh.

Staring at the cube, I recalled the blistered wasteland of my nightmares, the terrible gears, the burning steam. That voice roaring, then bubbling.

SSSO ClOSSSE.

The words slithered through my thoughts, and I knew I was *hearing* Kezsarak, not remembering him. The voice was smaller than it had been in my dream, muffled and constrained.

"Dillon, please!" I tore my eyes from the cube to stare pleadingly at his back. "Don't do this! He wants you to do this!"

Dillon's posture stiffened, but he didn't turn around. "Raza," he called. One of his men moved behind me.

A fist clubbed my ribs that were exposed between the rails, and I screamed in pain. Men chuckled, and when I opened my leaking eyes, a huge man stood between Jackie and me. He glared down at me from under beetled brows, daring me to say anything else.

"Dillon!" I shouted again. The demon in the box scared me more than any mere man.

Raza didn't strike me again, but Jackie gave a frightened squeak as the giant leveraged his foot on her throat.

"One more word," he growled and then held up a finger, daring me. "One."

He leaned a little more of his weight on Jackie, and she gave a gagging choke.

I glared up at him, imagining ripping up one of the plates from the floor and whacking him with it. Rage and terror stoked my heart to a thunderous pitch, and the most caustic curses I knew seethed in the back of my throat. I buried it all. Jackie's life depended on it.

I lapsed into silence and then turned my gaze to Dillon at the table.

"Very good." He held his ringed hand over the cube. "Now let's see about taming another beast."

I felt the energy of the cube, as interwoven and complex as the metals that wrapped it, respond to Dillon's call. The bands began to shift and slide with a soft hiss, gliding precisely, each movement corresponding perfectly with each other. Something stirred inside the cube. A rumble like thunder echoed from an impossible depth.

My mind and soul screamed, and I ground my teeth together, desperate to stop this before it was too late.

Trickles of soot and cinders rose from the cube.

It seemed as though it was a retelling of my nightmares in fits and starts. A cinder here and sooty curls of smoke there. The noise within the cube grew louder, less distant. It wasn't thunder but the throaty voice of a great engine. The sound grew near. More ash and burning fireflies emerged until a small cloud formed over the cube.

Within that cloud, I sensed a malignant awareness. I bit my lip to hold back a scream. He was nearly free.

Then the pitch shifted as Dillon altered his grip. The bands stilled. The engine's growl became a furious blast of anger as something screeched and ground within.

Dillon's arm was shaking as he held it out over the

cube. "All right, gallu." His voice trembled. "I've opened it as far as I'm going to. Let's talk."

The engine snarled and hissed to a chugging standstill. The ash and cinders seethed in the air. Dillon's hand steadied over the cube, the rings glowing in the light of the flashing cinders.

"Come now, don't be shy."

Cinders flared and danced, and in them formed a hellish pair of eyes, throwing ripples of hateful heat as they pressed to the fore.

RELEASE ME.

The sound pounded in my ears like the ringing of a hammer against an anvil. Raza winced, and Jackie whimpered, pressing her face to the floor.

"Nothing is for free," Dillon quipped, anxiety thinning his tone. "My employers insist we come to an arrangement before you are freed."

The eyes flared, and cinders sprayed in every direction. Dillon raised his free hand to shield his face.

RELEASE ME NOW, VERMIN.

"This 'vermin' is going to shut you back in the box forever if you don't cooperate," Dillon snarled. "Work with me or prepare for another eternity of prison, Kezsarak!"

The eyes narrowed into searing slits, and the ash thickened, only a few cinders sparked from the top. When he spoke again, it was sullenly. He almost sounded bored.

TERMS.

"I knew you could be reasonable." Dillon gestured to the table, where the guns lay. "I believe you know weapons of war when you see them. If the old stories are true, then you'll have no problem enhancing this small offering, as a show of good faith."

The smouldering eyes regarded the weapons.

AGREED, RELEASE ME.

Dillon actually laughed, and the eyes narrowed again. It like watching a time bomb counting down to detonation, and felt like all the air had been sucked from the factory.

"I don't think so," Dillon said, snorting. He waggled his outstretched fingers. "Now, please. Before I lose my temper."

The eyes remained hateful slits, but something reached over the table from the cloud. Kezsarak's will gave off waves of power, distorting everything. The power rested over the weapons, then sank into the metal like descending rain. Kezsarak's influence curdled the guns' resonance with a sour, prickly texture. With the barest hum, the dark metal of the guns shone with a red light.

COMPLETE, RELEASE ME.

Dillon eyed the weapons, no doubt sensing the wrongness in them just as I did.

"Some verification is in order." He snapped his fingers at the weapons. "Miggs, Jonesy, Damien, test these out."

Three men stepped forwards, each taking a weapon and a handful of ammunition. Moving away from the table, they began to load. The deviant auras livened as the first rounds were chambered, trembling with distorted, mutant life.

The men glanced at Dillon, hesitant.

"Get on with it, damn it!" Dillon levelled a finger at the man holding the handgun. "Jonesy first, and down the line. Step to, boys."

Jonesy looked like he would rather have dropped the pistol and run for his life. Sweat beaded on his pale forehead. He lifted the weapon in a two-handed grip and spread his feet. Aiming at one of the lorries, Jonesy's hands began to shake, as though he could feel the unfriendly evil brooding in the weapon.

"Shoot!" Dillon screamed.

A plume of scarlet erupted from the muzzle, and the door of the lorry exploded into gnarled, ribbons. It was almost comic, as the door peeled back like a trick cigar. A stunned silence followed as the last bits of metal and glass tumbled across the floor. It wasn't just the door on the side facing us that had been obliterated, but the one on the opposite side as well.

The men looked at each other in wonder, but Dillon was already jabbing his finger at the next man.

"Miggs, come on!"

Miggs hefted the shotgun to his shoulder, and after a single steadying breath, he pulled the trigger.

The damage struck from just above the front wheel well to the opposite wheel. It looked as though a giant, serrated blade ripped through the lorry, throwing part of the engine block into the air. The twisted hunk of metal spun, throwing off blackened pieces before it crashed to the ground.

Now the men were smiling.

When Damien opened up with the carbine, snapping off a trio of shots at the cab and the bed, metal flew, and the lorry's frame sagged, a broken, bifurcated shamble.

The goons clapped and hooted now in juvenile appreciation of the grandiose display. The three with demon-touched weapons shared wide, greedy smiles.

"That will do," Dillon cooed to the glowering demon. "I know quite a few parties who would be very interested in what you could do for them, my friend."

Kezsarak had given simple firearms the power of light artillery weapons. I shuddered with loathing. If he could multiply the destructive power of weapons, what would happen with a tank or a missile? What could he do to a nuclear bomb?

My mind was beggared by the horrific potential, and I

understood just how high the stakes were. Lowe hadn't prepared me for this. I had had no idea what I was getting into when I set about to stop Dillon.

The three stooges with hell-guns unloaded on another of the abandoned lorries, which nearly disintegrated entirely by the time they were finished. My ears rang with the immense noise but I could vaguely hear the men cheering and hollering at the display of destructive power. Dillon beamed like a proud parent watching his children at play.

This was an opportunity, I realised with a jolt. While they were distracted, I had to act. Do something. I wouldn't get another chance. I clenched my eyes shut, willing my abused eardrums to still so I could think.

Not knowing if Dillon held the rail around me with his power or not, I threw caution to the wind and hammered my own powers against the warped rail, pushing out and up all at once. The force of it dragged me to my feet. The coil released me, and I landed on quivering legs. Realizing with a shock that I was loose, with a backhand and a metal blow, I sent the rail spinning into Raza's face. It took him across the cheekbone, sending him flying backwards.

The apes were still all shooting and hooting when Dillon's head whipped around, and he saw me coming. He shrieked, but Kezsarak decided to make his own move for freedom.

Coalescing into tendrils, cinders and soot whipped out and wrapped around Dillon's outstretched wrist. One of the guns fired, and Miggs crumpled to his knees, both hands … simply missing. Then Jonesy was screaming, the twisted shotgun tumbled to the ground as his hands pawed at his bleeding face.

Dillon screamed. His whole body arched as he tried to free his wrist from Kezsarak's cask. I lunged towards him, but moving towards the cube was like wading through melted toffee.

RELEASE ME.

The tendrils of burning ash tightened, and there came a series of snaps from Dillon's wrist and elbow. His ringed hand lurched forwards. The rings of the Inconquo struck the cask, and each cuneiform etching flared with a sullen red light.

YESSS.

The exultant cry was a sonic hammer that drove me to my knees. Before flowing back into the cask, the soot and cinders released Dillon, who crumpled to the ground. The infernal engine revved to life again, and its pounding heartbeat shook the table as the cube shuddered and bounced.

FREEDOM.

Chapter Twenty-Three

I screamed through the pain of Kezsarak's roar, crawling on hands and knees towards Dillon. Seizing him by his shirt, I hauled him away as the table collapsed. Dillon's face was screwed up in pain, eyes pinched shut. His whole body was rigid, except for his arm, which he cradled. He didn't seem to notice I had him.

The cask swelled as it juddered about. A sound like metal screeching accompanied the thundering engine. The overhead lights flickered, buzzed, then went out, casting the foundry into darkness. Only the cube's baleful red glow illuminated the space.

The rings were still on Dillon's fingers, unharmed, though the skin on his hand was blackened and cracking. I touched the rings. They were hot but not enough to burn. Bracing a knee on Dillon's chest, I pulled both sets of rings from his fingers. They came off easily, as if too big for him.

Scrambling away, I clutched the rings to my chest. I slid the two sets of rings on my fingers. The broken halves clinked against one another. The rings slid over my knuckles loosely, then I felt them tighten as the supernatural alloy allied itself to its new owner. They now fit snugly, perfectly.

Glancing up at the cube, I watched in mute horror as the metal bands — now swollen and stretched beyond possibility — began to form a body. A vague impression of a wide humanoid shape with blade-like horns sweeping from the sides of a huge head. Soot and cinders swirled like a burning dervish. Through the rush of black and red, the smouldering eyes glared, ingots pulled fresh from hell's own forge.

TRAITOR, FAITHLESS.

Kezsarak loomed over me, at least twice the height of the tallest man I'd ever seen. Those burning eyes glowered a red darkness. Through rushing wisps of ash, a wide mouth gaped. I knew what awaited me inside. I could hear the gears whirring and clacking already.

My nightmare made real.

With the full set of rings on my fingers now, all the metal songs around me came through with strength and clarity. Even through the terror gnawing at my brain. I threw all the mental force I had into peeling up a wide section of the metal plating on the floor. My temples throbbed and the metal screamed as it broke free. Screws, shrapnel and dirt flew everywhere. With a catapulting arm, I sent it spinning like an enormous jagged disc.

He didn't even duck, letting the missile bury itself in his chest, face and neck. The metal plating began to melt and bubble, disappearing into his form … a welcomed addition. He took another step towards me, and I felt it reverberate through the floor. I backpedalled, cursing silently, as the last of my metal projectile vanished into the metal beast.

The gaping mouth rose at the corners.

Jackie screamed, and I swept the space for her. My

heart lurched as I saw her crawling away from the demon towards the shadows. Her gag was loose around her neck, hanging like a kerchief. Her hands were still bound in front of her. Thinking Dillon's men might catch her, I scanned for them, eyes wide. But in the short time I'd engaged with Kezsarak, Dillon and his men had vanished, leaving me here to deal with the mess.

Every stride of Kezsarak's equalled four of mine, but he seemed in no hurry, enjoying the certainty of my destruction.

Jackie staggered to her feet and ran a few steps before turning to scream my name.

"Run!" I shouted back. "Get out of here!"

She stood there torn and trembling. Looking at Kezsarak helped her find her legs, and with a sob, she ran. She disappeared into the gloom behind the vehicles and vats. I was relieved to watch her go.

Kezsarak plodded for me as I backed up, mind whirring like a top.

Sensing the rails running along the floor and the great buckets overhead, I cast about for inspiration. This place was full of metal. Find something to use, Ibby!

Kezsarak took another step. There was a soft jingle from the chains, barely audible over the grinding gears inside his maw.

Desperately, I grasped a long piece of tempered steel beam where it lay on the flatbed of an old truck, unsure if I could even lift it. Throwing an espresso machine had nearly knocked me unconscious.

The rings amplified my power beyond what I expected. It was like wrestling a python, but the beam responded with greater fluidity. Like a rearing snake, it swung up behind Kezsarak and swayed there. His huge horned head turned to look.

Screaming with effort, I swung the immense tendril of steel like a bat, driving the demon onto one knee. My fingers curled, and the beam encircled Kezsarak, holding him fast. His burning gaze flared in outrage, but I squeezed the coil even tighter, clenching my teeth so hard I wondered if they'd crack.

AMUSING.

Pain hammered through my head. I wasn't done yet. Keeping hold of the beam, I reached for the chains holding the industrial buckets. *Flex.* The chains swayed and the bucket tipped. Decades-old dust and slag rained down.

"If you liked that, you're gonna love this," I snarled and broke the links holding the bucket.

Kezsarak looked up to watch the meteoric fall of the bucket. His limbs were still enclosed behind the beam, which had begun to bubble and melt.

Like a huge bell, the bucket plummeted, smashing down on Kezsarak and trapping him inside. The impact shook the floor, and my legs splayed out for balance. Hand outstretched, I unleashed my power on the bucket. Old, crotchety steel cracked as my breath came in gasps, and spots danced in front of my eyes. I kept pressing, kept squeezing, until the old steel buckled and imploded.

I felt a vibration through the floor and up my legs. My eyes widened. The bucket shimmered red and gave a bass hum. Its resonance putrefied in my mind's grip, and it was like holding something rotten. When I squeezed harder, it exploded.

The blast sent me rolling, and a wave of pressure washed over me, sucking on my inner ears. Glowing shards of metal spun through the air, jamming into the ceiling, walls and floor. In their wake came a tide of grit and dust. The ceramic lining turned sandstorm as it exploded from the annihilated bucket.

VERY AMUSING.

Laying on my side, I raised a hand against the stinging wind. A storm of smouldering darkness came striding out of the tumbling dust devils.

Crawling to my feet, I held my hands out, palms down. With a wave of energy, I sucked the rivets out of the floor. I'd no more called on them, then Kezsarak's own power took them from me. They tightened away as if drawing back to fire. I did my best baseball dive and slide out of the way, but slivers of metal peppered my right side. The jacket and jeans were some protection, but several hot stings burned across my shoulder and thigh.

MY TURN.

A horrible screeching sound filled the air, and I looked up to see a lorry lurch forwards. Flat tyres flapping on mangled rims, the vehicle came for me, an infernal red glow suffusing the whole frame. Rattling and pounding, it picked up speed. I was about to be crushed.

I reached out to a length of chain on the tracks above. With a jingling hiss, they snaked down but the ceiling was nearly half a dozen metres up. The hellish corona blinding me as the lorry neared, I kept my hand outstretched. The instant the cold steel touched my fingers, I grabbed a hold. I sent a panicked, wordless command, and the chain yanked me up into the air. The lorry tore past, the tips of my trainers skidding across the pitted cab.

My arm and shoulder screaming, I flew until I was swinging in a nest of chains on the ceiling. Grabbing another handful of chains, I looped my legs through some others, taking the pressure off my shoulder.

Below, the lorry smashed into the wall, the rusted metal crumpling in on itself. It detonated. A crimson glare flashed. Curls of metal sheeting and hunks of concrete spun through the air. Blasted by another rush of hot air and stinging sparks, I swung there, chains squeaking.

From my perch, I saw a gaping hole in the side of the building. Girders, I-beams as thick as me, jutted from the crumbling concrete like exposed ribs. Beyond the ragged breach was the tangled, rain-slicked yard, and barely visible, the gnarled line of the fence.

RUN, TRAITOR.

I looked down and saw Kezsarak's burning eyes narrowed in amusement. A huge, scaly arm swept towards the wound, and the girders began to glow and steam. An almost animal-like groan shook the wall, and I watched the portal widen invitingly.

RUN, SO I MIGHT CHASE YOU.

I tore my eyes from the temptation and glared at the demon. Behind him stretched the imprints of his footsteps, smoking pits of molten metal. The sludge ran and bubbled, buckling the floor plates. I imagined those same burning footprints following me down the streets of Greenwich, people screaming as the gallu spread ruin in his wake.

I couldn't let that happen. Damn it, I was a guardian after all.

"I'm not done with you yet, big boy," I shouted and dropped clear, fists wrapped in lengths of chain.

I dropped, thrilling in the momentary weightlessness. My shoulders screamed with the effort as I drew on the interconnected metal running from the chain to the track. I heard a clank and groan overhead.

The swing carried me down on a collision course with his face. Kezsarak reached for me from the ashen cloud. At the last second, I mentally yanked the chains backwards. My shoulders popped as I whiplashed away from the gallu's grip, but the noise was swallowed by the resounding groan as the gear assembly swung free of its track. At first, gravity, then the rings, amplified the fury, shivering up the chains as the massive collection of gears spiralled opposite me. I spun by as the tank-sized hammer crashed into Kezsarak's chest.

The sound was a gratifying, bone-deep 'whump' as the demon flew backwards, huge body ragdolling across the foundry floor. Head over heels, he pitched into one of the vats, trailing burning streamers of soot.

I landed heavy, but rolled into it and came up howling. "How's that for running, you bastard!"

Like tarry fumes over an imminent eruption, Kezsarak's cloud roiled above the basin. He was down, but far from out.

Overhead, more giant buckets swung like mute cathedral bells. One hadn't been enough, but if at first you don't succeed …

I threw my ringed hand out and raked at the chains at the limit of my reach. The weary links gave up their decades-old burdens. The buckets crashed into the basin, scattering soot and cinders. One stomach-fluttering gong after another, they impacted, and I was already looking for something else to hit him with. Something bigger, something harder.

I never got the chance as a thundering roar rose out of the basin, and I felt for the first time the true extent of Kezsarak's furious power. He reached out to the girders framing the building, the vast skeletal structure. I wrapped a mental hold around one huge I-beam, then realised he had a hold of *all* of them, even through layers of metal sheeting and thick concrete. He was tuning them to a single apocalyptic note, and the air vibrated with their response. The overhead lights snapped and sparked off, a sullen red glow suffusing everything.

Instinctively, I ripped up a swath of floor sheeting and cocooned myself with it, forming a metallic hamster ball. The red glow leaked through the seams, flaring and suddenly winking out. I had half a second to hear my breath rasping in the dark and to brace myself within the metallic egg, before the world erupted.

Bouncing and spinning, I seemed to be travelling in every direction at once. Impacts across the reshaped sheeting rattled and banged, but I tumbled on. Here and there something sharp and blazing hot would punch through, but whatever they were flew by so fast I didn't have a chance to think about how close they'd come to skewering me. I was far too busy just holding the perforated shell intact.

Something which felt like a falling skyscraper came down on the shell, and it exploded. I flew clear, riding the last fragment of sheeting like a saucer. Skittering across the remains of the toppled walls and collapsed ceiling, my metal ride screamed to a halt.

My body ached like one huge bruise as I climbed off the sheeting, the joints that weren't painfully locked felt dangerously loose instead. I took in a breath and choked on the clouds of swirling powdered concrete. As I hacked up a throat full of cement dust, I couldn't hear anything aside from a dull ringing as it rose in volume and pitch. For a few gagging breaths, that perpetual chime was all I knew.

When I spat out a mouthful of grey sludge, it gave a wet slap on the ruined metal. The first sign my hearing was returning. A humid wind cleared some of the air, and I looked up. A handful of cold stars winked at me between dark banks of cloud. The ruin of the foundry settled with a final dusty sigh. The rain had stopped, I realized randomly.

The air was still for a beat, then Kezsarak's roar drove

the silence away like a splitting maul.

I spun, still reeling and horrified, as he pounded towards me, rubble blackening in his wake. One hand trailed swirling ash, as his fist drew jagged spurs of metal from the rubble. Shards rocketed towards him from everywhere, drawn to the enormous magnet of his fist. Three strides from me, and his fist was a spiked wrecking ball. Two strides, and that wrecking ball raised overhead.

My heart in my throat, I sent the sheeting I'd ridden spinning up into his burning face, then did a panicked dive to the side. A crater opened where I once stood. Screaming as I scrambled up and away, my ankles turned painfully on the treacherous terrain. My mind reached out for metal, but what wasn't part of Kezsarak was buried under shattered concrete. He was nearly upon me again. Every hair on my neck and forearms stood on end as I anticipated pain and destruction. My throat was screaming with my breath feeling both burned and frozen.

A hunk of rubble rolled under my foot, and I stumbled just as Kezsarak pounced.

A huge, diagonal blow scythed towards me, and I did my best to twist away, my mind screaming for metal to block him. A spur on his wreckage-swollen fist was going to catch me, heading for my left shoulder. Out of time to react, muscles burning, I winced before the fatal collision.

Something hot, almost scalding splashed across my arm and shoulder as the swing impossibly whistled by. No. Not by. *Through.*

But the hot wetness wasn't my blood. I gaped at where I should have been split in two, my jaw dropping in disbelief. Molten iron coated my entire arm and shoulder. Its aura, still tainted by Kezsarak, called to me, pleading, and instinctively I responded.

The metal flowed and moulded itself over my arm and

shoulder to form a resilient second skin. I didn't have time to stare at my new bionic-looking arm. It was immediately put to the test as Kezsarak's hammering fist came down. I turned my reinforced shoulder into the blow, metal-sheathed arm warding my face. The force of the impact turned all my senses momentarily to static, As I staggered back from the blow, the liquid metal spread, coating more of my body.

Kezsarak glared, eyes narrowed. His voice came out in that insidious, hair-raising hiss.

TRAITOR.

Fresh metal slid across my torso to coat my other arm. I straightened, both iron-shod arms raised in a boxer's guard.

INSECT.

I bared my teeth, feet grinding in the rubble to brace my legs. The liquid metal crawled up my neck and down over my ribcage, lending strength wherever it touched.

A dark, mocking laugh rumbled as he lunged forwards, fist sweeping down to flatten me. Crossing my arms over my head, I took the blow, wincing and preparing for immense pain, if not death. The incredible blow stopped dead with a thunk, but the shock of it shuddered down my abused shoulders through my body and into my feet.

Lifting my gaze and seeing my own amazement reflected in his burning eyes, the corners of my mouth lifted in a grim smile.

"Come on!" I snarled, digging deep even as I felt him leveraging his huge body to crush me. "That all you got?"

Kezsarak's eyes narrowed, seething with venomous hate. His malignant intention slithered down towards me, wrapping itself around my body like a constrictor. Goose bumps rose where his mind trailed by. My new metal casing hardened against him, rebellious to his intent.

FAITHLESS.

The words bubbled out like blood from a deep wound. I looked up in horror to see shards of metal encasing his fist and giving a deadly red shimmer. An instant later, the metal sheathing soaked my arms with the same fevered glow, its aura giving a mournful chorus. I sank to a knee as I felt his growing influence approaching critical mass. With a cry that was part scream and part wail, I mentally gripped the metal encasing me and threw it sideways. My internal organs and bones compressed as my body flew through the air.

Kezsarak's fist descended and the metal seemed to detonate. Not for the first time that night, my world became a spinning kaleidoscope of pain and confused sensation as I tumbled across the broken ground. I pitched up at last against something hard and rough.

My head still spinning, I placed my hands against my resting place and understood. I lay against a broken boulder of concrete with a few buried deposits of metal I could faintly sense. My mind still sluggish and muddy, I feebly reached out to the metal, not even sure what I was going to do with it.

FOOL.

The rebuke came with another flicker of his power. There was a crackle and a screech as something exploded. I covered my face to keep the shrapnel from my eyes. Shrapnel peppered my arms and torso, tinging off my armour. When the eruptions ceased, the thundering of Kezsarak stood over me, eyes narrowed.

I let out a gasp of despair. I was exhausted and out of ideas. I was surrounded by metals, but Kezsarak's power over them was stronger than mine.

AVENGED AT LAST.

A huge hand reached towards me from the soot.

Heaving myself into a roll, I narrowly avoided his grasp. A wave of heat washed over me as his huge hand clamped on air. With what felt like my last ounce of adrenaline, I scrambled to my feet. Skirting around the boulder, I slid in the dust, chest heaving. Ducking behind another heap of wreckage, I leaned my back against the rubble, my eyes clenched shut. I needed to think.

With a gasp, I opened my eyes and made a mad dash for one of the other buckets that had fallen when I broke the chain. Sliding in the dust, I leaned my back against the old vat and squeezed my eyes shut.

WEAKLING.

Thunderous footsteps approached. I looked down at the rings where they hugged all four fingers of my right hand. The crack where Lowe had broken them … the crack! They had been *broken*. Pinching my fingers close together, the two broken halves of the gauntlet of rings came together, almost disappearing entirely. I sucked in an astonished breath.

Keszarak batted away the old kettle like it was a balloon. My hair whipped around my face in the blast of heat. I didn't look up, only down at the rings.

Heat, I directed the metal lining the broken halves. *Melt.*

The strange alloy grew shiny along the seam. Little tendrils of steam wisped from my fingers. The metal was hot enough to melt through bone, but did not harm me. Closing my two middle fingers, I pressed the hot sides together.

Fuse. Weld. Be whole again, the way the first Inconquo made you.

The two sides of the rings melded. They became one solid gauntlet, a thick bar of supernatural power across my fist.

I looked up as Keszarak's heat came over me — heat

that could not burn me. He reached for me again. Covering his spreading fingers and stretching arms was a skin, like Dillon's charred hand, but rough and jagged. I looked up into those red eyes, unafraid. A power throbbed on my hand and through my body, unlike anything I'd felt before.

Keszarak paused.

In that stillness, familiar chords reverberated. They were strings I knew. Clear and low, the song of iron sang from deep within that craggy arm. With a soft mental caress, I sang back to it.

A sharp, crackling sound raced up Kezsarak's arm, and the engine within gave a grinding snarl. Inches from my face, the fingers curled inwards, the skin thickening. I met the demon's burning gaze.

In those hot, hellish eyes. I saw fear, and that filled me with fresh strength.

The iron within him had answered me.

Casting into the storm of swirling ash, I discovered other metals, languishing under Kezsarak's insane will. Tin, mercury, lead, copper, silver and even gold. All had endured the betrayal of Kezsarak, who'd warped them into ruin and cruelty. They cried out for one who knew their ancient tongue, one who could remind them they did not need to serve the treacherous will of a mad demon.

They cried out for an Inconquo.

I made a fist with my right hand, lifting the gauntlet. Kezsarak recoiled, staggering back, his movements stiff with the iron's insurgence.

Closing my eyes, I let the Inconquo take over.

As though they were living things, the metals within the beast mourned. Ancient compounds, beautiful and strong, communed with my blood. I could taste them, sense them, hear their music. I whispered to them, reminding them they were beautiful and good. They could be exorcised from the one who controlled them. Haunted metals. They could be free.

With my ageless will to bolster them, they rose up as one within Kezsarak, rejecting his control. Cinder and soot whirled inwards as the demon twisted in on himself. Mutiny roiled within him as the metals broke free. A pearly stream of metallic liquid oozed from the cracks in his body, seeping from within and draining his power. Bright coppery tendrils curled across the floor, threading their way through the dirt away from Kezsarak.

The engine of my nightmares shrieked as crank shafts twisted and gears splintered. The cinders were gone, and the ash drifted down in thin ribbons. The malevolent storm slowly cleared, leaving a shadow of the thing he'd been before malice and grief polluted him.

Tiny streams of silver and gold crawled and flowed, spreading like a star slowly exploding. The metals began to glow, their light increasing as Kezsarak's dimmed. Darker grey ribbons rolled and tumbled gleefully, drawn to where I stood.

Kezsarak's form cleared as the ash and cinders dwindled. Bovine legs of beaten copper supported a wide, muscled belly of sculpted lead. Above this was a man's powerful chest in burnished tin and two mighty arms of iron. Resplendent above the body was a thoughtful, bearded face of dark gold, which bore silver horns sweeping from proud temples. The eyes, which no longer burned but glimmered, were pools of mercury cupped within golden sockets.

He was primal and yet somehow refined. Life still glimmered in those quicksilver eyes, sad, bitter and broken.

END ME, INCONQUO.

The voice was so small now.

PLEASE.

Ancestors from ages past created this monster. In spite of everything that had passed between us, I pitied him.

"Sleep," I said softly, and I used my power to press the thought home.

For an instant, he resisted. His resentment, grief and shame flashed against my mind. Then he surrendered, letting the power of the rings bear him into the depths of himself.

Smooth and soft, the statued form of Kezsarak shrank and melted. A gentle implosion, until only the cuneiformed bands slid into place. A few moments later, the cask rested on the foundry floor. Still once more.

I let out a long, low breath. My metallic armour had vanished, whether it had retreated into my body or joined the melted metal on the floor, I didn't know.

Looking down, I gave a start. With Keszarak contained within his cube, the only light in the space now came in as either moonlight, through cracks in the faraway ceiling, or from the glowing wet metal, which had curled around my feet. Somehow, the silvers, golds, greys, coppers and reds of those metals had leaked across the floor to make a shape. The shape surrounded me on all sides, laying on the surface around me, like an elaborate metallic sun.

Squatting, I reached my hand out to touch it, and I felt the heat and the relief within the sun's beads of reformed matter. Standing again, I stared at the shape, realising I could read it. It was not a language but a symbol, and somehow, I understood what it meant. A simple emotion: gratitude.

Picking up the cask, I was relieved to find that — despite what it contained — it was light.

I was even more thankful for that fact when, straightening, I heard distant sirens and realised I needed to leave.

Chapter Twenty-Four

Kezsarak's cube under my arm, my feet slapping across the marshy plain, I ran from the foundry as fast as my abused body could manage. Every muscle and joint ached, and my left leg didn't want to cooperate. My skin stung in places from cuts and punctures. My clothes were still damp and clung miserably to my body, shredded and ruined.

Police vehicles cut a soggy track across the park towards the main gate as I slipped through a gap in the fence. They'd find broken firearms along with mangled old machinery. Maybe even a few bodies of Dillon's men. In the chaos, I didn't know what had happened to them. I wondered what the police would conclude from it all. I could always read about it in the news.

My body hurt from all the abuse, but my stomach growled ferociously. I could murder a taco or ten.

A grove at the edge of the field gave me cover so I slowed to look back and see if I was being pursued. Police officers swarmed from their vehicles. No one seemed to notice me so far, but it was likely someone would follow my tracks.

The night was dark with patches of clouds, the ground slippery and wet. It made for slow going through the thin patch of timber. More than once, I stumbled over a root or ran into a low branch. My leg muscles burned and begged me to stop and sit. The trees soon thinned, and I arrived at the road which swept around the bottom of the park and into Greenwich's residential area.

Muttering and wincing, I reached inside the jacket to draw out my phone. I had the map of central London downloaded offline. Even if the foundry was off the edge of the map, I might be able to get my bearings, then get to Covent Garden Station and back to Lowe. I kicked myself for not thoroughly thinking through an exit strategy.

I nearly burst into tears when I saw the screen had splintered and the mobile wouldn't respond. I chucked the useless phone back in my pocket. With nothing else to do, I limped down the side of the road.

A short time later, a vehicle rounded the curve. I had a brief surge of panic at the bright flashing lights until realising it was an ambulance. Too exhausted to find somewhere to hide, I stopped walking and watched the vehicle slow.

A woman in a green ambulance uniform, complete with cap and windslicker, leapt out. She hustled towards me, took me by the arm and began to lead me to the ambulance.

"I don't want to go," I grunted. "I'm fine."

"To hell with what you want!" she huffed, her grip unflinching. "I've been this way twice already. How long do you think an ambulance can circle a neighbourhood inconspicuously?"

Squinting at the woman, I watched as her face shifted into that of someone I knew. She smiled and continued to haul me towards the back of the ambulance. I didn't resist.

"Daria?" I said, huskily.

"There's plenty of gauze and disinfectant. Plenty of water. But if you get into the narcotics, I'm turning this boat around. Mark my words."

The rear door swung open, and there on a stretcher, blanket around her shoulders, sat Jackie Davies. She rose, blankets tumbling, and helped me to the bench in the back.

"Oh, Ibby," she croaked. Tears poured down her face as she threw a blanket over my shoulders. "You're alive." She put her arms around me, and we melted into one another.

I let my eyes droop shut. "We're alive," I echoed, my breath hitching. Keszarak's cask slipped from my grasp and landed on the floor, cushioned by the blanket draped over me. I didn't have the energy to pick it up. Let it stay there for now.

Dary closed the door, and a moment later the ambulance began to move. Jackie bent and produced a water bottle. She unscrewed the cap and handed it to me. I drank greedily, washing the taste of ash out of my mouth. We swayed as the vehicle carried us out of the park and onto the London streets.

"Ibby?" Jackie's voice was soft and tremulous.

I screwed the cap back on the bottle. "Yeah?"

"I'm beginning to see why you doubt my taste in men."

I chuckled a dry laugh and gave my enlightened one a hug.

I SAT on a bench in Museum Station commons letting Daria remove shrapnel from my arm. Jackie sat nearby, staring around moon-eyed.

"You get used to it," I told her with a wince. "Ow."

"That's the last piece," Daria said, dropping the metal bit into a bowl.

"No, she will not!" Lowe thundered, as he materialised from the aether. "Ibby, this is a junction between the realms of the spiritual and the material, not a youth hostel!"

Jackie's eyes were in danger of coming out of her head. "The ghost?" she whispered, hoarsely and pointed.

On the way to Covent Garden, I'd given her a crash course in my new life. She was still adjusting. Overall, I think she was doing remarkably well, though Lowe's sudden appearance and bad temper weren't helping things.

"Yes, I'm the ghost," Lowe huffed and then flapped his long arms. "BOO!"

Jackie blinked and recoiled but made no sign she was about to run away screaming.

"Lowe, don't be rude," Daria chided as she swabbed and bandaged my arm. "They've been through enough tonight."

"But they can't stay here, not long term, at least," he pressed.

"I don't want to go home," Jackie mumbled. "I won't feel safe there."

"Ibby was here only a few days, and this place was a state," Lowe went on as if he couldn't hear. "Soot and ash on the upholstery. Dirty laundry in the corners. With two of you, it will be exponentially worse."

"Wait a minute." I slid forwards, jaw first. "First, I was under psychic assault by a demon. Second, I was attacked at my flat, and third, we can't stay here because you're afraid we'll be too messy?"

Lowe drew himself up, smartly. "Ibby, I care for you deeply, and if you ever *need* a place to stay, I will of course oblige. But you are living, and so is Ms Davies. You need to be out there … well … being alive. Not in here avoiding life."

"Like you?" Dary remarked, dryly.

"Precisely," Lowe answered without a hint of shame. "Besides, I'm going to be busy with our new … friend." His eyes slid to Kezsarak's cube, where it sat at the foot of the obelisk.

"It is going to be delicate work. It's for the best that the only person around to get hurt is a dead man."

I wanted to argue further, but he was right. If something happened, and Kezsarak needed containing, I wouldn't be far, but living here was out of the question. All the coming and going to get food and necessities would eventually draw attention and put Winterthür on our trail.

"Let's get a place together," Jackie piped up. "I have money enough to keep us afloat for a while. I don't particularly want to live alone anymore."

"That's a splendid idea," Lowe said, enthusiastically.

I met her eye, and we shared a nod. It was good to have a friend.

"Well," I sighed as I stood up, my body patched and bandaged. "I'm going to need to find a job. Archaeology is no longer in the future of Ms Bashir."

"I'm sorry, love," Jackie said earnestly.

"I wouldn't assume that yet." Dary got to her feet, shouldering her kit. "If you'll remember, I used to have connections in that sphere. Give me a little time, and we'll see what shakes out."

I gawked at her, torn between hope and self-protecting suspicion. "You could really do that?"

Dary winked. "Give me a little time — is all I'm saying."

Spontaneously, I wrapped her up in a hug. At first, she was too surprised to react but by degrees she returned it.

"Thank you," I whispered.

"Thank *you*." She held me at arm's length, sporting a mysterious smile.

"Excellent," Lowe said, clasping his hands together. "You ladies are moving out. Ibby will get her future back. I get to rehabilitate an ancient demon ..."

"I need to call my Uncle Iry," I added. "Let him know I'm okay. My last message had a 'goodbye' type feeling."

"Yes, that too," Lowe remarked, mildly, then cleared his throat. "About, Mr Sark ... I believe he is still at large."

To our surprise, Dary chuckled. "Oh, I wouldn't worry about him." Her smile turned wicked. "I made a couple of calls. Sark won't be bothering any of us for some time."

Epilogue

Dillon Sark was out of breath from taking the stairs two at a time. He sagged briefly against the wall as he reached the roof of a small apartment complex on the south side.

His right arm hung limply at his side and throbbed terribly. He couldn't stand to look at it. The flesh was swollen and bruised. He needed medical attention, but it was too risky.

He'd been exposed, and for those who worked with Winterthür, that meant only one thing.

He'd arrived at his penthouse in Battersea Park and found it crawling with Metro bobbies. After a moment of eavesdropping, he discovered they had him labelled as a domestic terrorist or arms dealer. He was on his way to becoming the most wanted man in London, if not the UK.

He'd slipped away then, his mind racing. The police were not his primary concern, though they did complicate things. It was his employer that had him worried. Disgraced members of Winterthür very quickly became former members … by way of execution. He ought to know; he'd carried out the deed himself several times.

He needed to get out of London for the time being, figure out a way to get back in good standing. He wasn't sure what that would look like, but he was determined to see it done. He needed time to think.

He was a clever man after all.

What had followed his flight from Battersea Park was an exercise in frustration. Safehouse after safehouse was compromised. Bobbies swarmed every retreat. The idiot police couldn't have discovered his safehouses themselves. He'd been betrayed. Sold out.

The roof was a very old hiding spot and offered nothing more than a hidden duffel bag with some new ID, money and a change of clothes. It had been so long since he'd prepped it, he'd nearly forgotten about it entirely.

He rushed towards an air conditioning unit, stolen screwdriver in hand, but he stopped when he saw the panel was hanging loosely from a single screw. Years of paranoia set his hair on end, and he whirled around.

A beautiful woman in a dark coat stood next to the stairwell door. Her arrival had been completely soundless. She gave him a sharp smile and winked at the upraised screwdriver. A dingy, black duffel bag sat at her feet.

"Come now, Archy," she purred. "That's no way to greet a friend."

Sark swore. "That's mine," he growled, nodding towards the bag. "And, I hate that name."

"We should never be ashamed of where we come from, Archy," she chided and gave a cold little laugh. "Relax, I'm here to help."

She tossed the bag at Dillon's feet.

He squatted and rifled through the contents. Everything was present, but there was something extra. He drew out a small envelope of heavy stock. There was handwriting on the front.

With love, D. Tehom.

There was something hard and small inside.

"What's this?" he asked, as he straightened.

"It's your way back in, Archy," she explained. "This is what gets you back under the sheltering wing of Winterthür."

Dillon looked at the envelope and then back at the woman, his eyes narrowing. "And what does it get you?"

The woman's eyes flashed with something dangerous. "Don't ask questions you don't want the answers to."

Sark raised the envelope and tore it open with his teeth. He fished out a tiny stone cylinder. It had holes bored through its sides and cuneiform inscribed on either end.

"What's this?"

But when he looked up, he was alone with only the wail of sirens drifting up from the wet streets below.

End of Book One

The final book in this duopoly, *Metal Angel, Rings of the Inconquo*, Book 2 will be out before the end of 2019.

Also by A.L. Knorr

The Elemental Origins Series

Born of Water

Born of Fire

Born of Earth

Born of Æther

Born of Air

The Elementals

Mira's Return Trilogy

Returning

Falling

Surfacing

The Siren's Curse Series

Salt & Stone

Salt & the Sovereign

Salt & the Sisters

Elemental Novellas

Pyro, A Fire Novella

Heat, A Fire Novella

The Kacy Chronicles

Descendant

Ascendant

Combatant

Transcendent

Also by A.D. Schneider

The Warring Realm Series

War-Born (Book 1)

War-Torn (Book 2)

War-Sworn (Book 3)

Made in the USA
Monee, IL
10 April 2020

25084200R00154